The Most Important Decisions You Will Make Over 50

A ROADMAP TO A JOYFUL RETIREMENT THROUGH SOCIAL SECURITY MAXIMIZATION

Sandy Morris

Sandy Morris Financial
TAMPA, FLORIDA

Sandy Morris/Sandy Morris Financial
10015 Gallant Lane
Tampa, FL 33625
www.sandymorrisfinancial.com

Book layout ©2013 BookDesignTemplates.com

Ordering information:
For details, contact the address above.

The Most Important Decisions You Will Make Over 50/ Sandy Morris.
—1st ed.
ISBN-13: 978-1515389323

Contents

To my mother, Sherry, the most patient, loving mother a girl could have, and my father, Bill, who help me understand "what doesn't kill you, does make you stronger," and whose tough love taught me how to be resourceful and appreciate grace.

Preface

"A wise man makes his own decisions, an ignorant man follows the public opinion."

~ Grantland Rice

Every day when the sun comes up, the alarm goes off and you place your feet on the floor to begin a new day, you start making decisions. What to wear? What to eat for breakfast? Some decisions are pre-made. If you are still in the working phase of life, reporting for work is an obligation, not an option. Other decisions, however, require choices. Dining out this weekend? There's one that may require some discussion and deductive reasoning.

During the years between 21 and 50, we are in what I call the "fast lane" years, when we will encounter such major intersections as what career to train for and follow, whether and whom to marry, whether to rent or buy a home. Some decisions we will make actively and others we will make passively, but those choices will be made one way or the other. In my opinion, it's better to control our future than to allow the events of our future to control us. That's what this book is about. How to maintain a pro-active attitude toward the important decisions we will face after we hit the half-century mark.

Why 50? Why that age? Because it is a very pivotal time. I think you will see evidence of that as you continue reading. For most of us, 50 is when we start to come face-to-face with our own mortality. It's when we begin changing lanes, so to speak, from the fast lane of building wealth and growing our families and our careers into the more sedentary lane of preservation and planning for what comes after we reach the pinnacle we are scaling. From a financial point of view, caution is in order. Life after 50 is characterized by several major life decisions — junctions at which a wrong turn could cost us hundreds of thousands of dollars either in actual losses or missed opportunities. It's those decisions I want to talk with you about in this book.

Education, Knowledge Expel Fear

One theme you will pick up on as you proceed through these pages is that education and knowledge expel fear. Let's face it: the idea of making important money decisions is enough to cause paralysis in some people. "What if I get it wrong?" they worry to themselves. So they opt to do nothing, or even worse, let someone else decide for them. As you will see as you read on, my recommendation is to replace that fear with confidence through knowledge. Most fear is born from lack of understanding what's in front of us. I read somewhere that it has something to do with a million-year-old fight or flight response. If you don't understand something, you can't tackle it so the next response is to fear and run away from it. I don't know about that. But here's a novel approach to the life decisions that come at us as we approach midlife and beyond. Instead of fearing what we don't understand, why not study and understand the unknown until we know it and know it well? Then our paralysis is replaced by confidence and a sense of security — simple byproducts of bridging the knowledge gap.

Our Financial Journey

Financially speaking, our life is a quest — a journey of sorts — with a starting point and a destination. Our starting point is typically our first job and our destination is retirement. For most folks, the goal is to set aside enough so they can enjoy their golden years in relative comfort without having to worry about running out of money or becoming a burden to others. Decisions we make at intersections we encounter along the way can determine not only how soon we reach retirement, but also the quality of life that awaits us there.

Even in this age of information and enlightenment, there are too many retirees and soon-to-be retirees who are still uninformed about some key principles of how to plan their journey toward retirement. Some are doing what I call "tail light" navigating — that is simply following the tail lights of the person in front of them — taking advice from relatives, friends and co-workers, many of whom mean well, but simply aren't as well informed as they think they are. Sorry, but it's true. Some suffer from information overload. The airwaves are choked with experts spewing conflicting opinions because it's good theatre for the networks. The print media is so awash with books and magazines on the subject of investing that it's impossible to process it with any real understanding. Go to your local bookstore and visit the magazine counter. The size of the money section will startle you. Some just throw up their hands in confusion and postpone planning for their retirement. Understandable, but not really an option, folks.

As you read on, you will find that I have no axes to grind, turf to defend, ideas to sell, philosophy to push, nor do I want to point any fingers at those who do. Hey, it's a free country, after all, and everybody has a right to his or her opinion. What I do have are experiences to share, and I want to give you an uncluttered road map that will display all of your options. You may see some concepts that, while they are by no means secret, are less advertised methods of acquiring and preserving wealth and distributing it during retirement. That's another reason I wanted to write this book. There are some dangers on the road to retirement that you need to know about, and hopefully I can illuminate them for you.

CHAPTER ONE

The Retirement Stampede

"As the baby boomers like me are retiring and getting ready to retire, they will spend whatever it takes — and they're the wealthiest genera- tion in our country — to make themselves live an enjoyable life in their retirement years."

~ David Rubenstein

Here is a statistic that, when I first read it, made me think of the Tampa Bay Times Forum. I will tell you why in a moment. The statistic that caught my eye is that somewhere in the neighborhood of 10,000 peo- ple will turn 65 each day for approximately the next two decades. It's the baby boom generation coming of age.

Officially, to be a baby boomer, you have to have been born between 1946 and 1964. So the oldest members of this group started turning 65 in 2011 at the rate of 10,000 per day, according to the Pew Research Center (PRC). The baby boom generation got its name from the pro- nounced spike in the national birth rate that occurred when the soldiers who fought World War II came home after the war ended in 1945 and started raising families. Oh yes! What put me in mind of the Tampa Bay Times Forum, an arena near where I live in Tampa, Florida, is that the capacity of this local sports venue is slightly more than 21,000. So nationwide, the number of baby boomers turning 65 every two days would just about fill that arena. By 2030, when all members of the baby boom generation have reached that 65, fully 18 percent of the nation will be at least that age or older, says the PRC.

Who would have imagined that the generation that gave us rock and roll, flower power, the Rolling Stones and The Beatles would one day be lining up for Medicare and Social Security at such an alarming rate? But don't you dare tell boomers that they are old. The PRC survey said that the typical boomer doesn't believe old age starts until age 72. Most of those surveyed perceive themselves as nine years younger than their actual age. Sixty is the new 40, they say. Age is only a number.

The aging of the boom generation is having a dramatic economic effect on America and the phenomenon will continue, experts tell us. In 1970, when the oldest baby boomers were in their early 20s, the total publicly-held national debt was about $283 billion, or about 28 percent of the Gross Domestic Product. As I write this, the national debt clock is spinning like an odometer out of control, having so far racked up a $17 trillion debt, writing IOUs that children and grandchildren of the boom generation will have to pay.

It is a fact that members of the baby boom generation are living longer than did their parents and grandparents. Those past generations, on average, retired at 65 and lived until age 72. That's a seven-year retirement. In those days, they counted on their Social Security and likely a pension to see them through that seven-year span. Today's retirees, on the other hand, have to plan for a 20- or 25-year retirement income. Most of them have no pensions and live under the shadow of rising health care costs. The average lifespan has increased to the mid-eighties and the probability that one spouse will live to age 90 is 50.3 percent, according to the PRC.

So as shocking as it may seem, the folks who brought us rock and roll and coined the phrase "never trust anyone over 30" are now ready for retirement. And do they understand what awaits them? Not really, it seems. The National Association of Insurance Commissioners (NAIC) recently did a survey and found that, out of the 337 boomers they interviewed, only 36 percent knew they were eligible for Medicare at age 65. Twenty-one percent thought Medicare coverage began at age 62; 9 percent said age 67; 6 percent said age 59 ½. Twenty-eight percent said they just didn't know.

Maybe you see why I find these numbers bothersome. If baby boomers are basing their plans for retirement on those mistaken notions, I wonder how many other aspects of retirement they are confused about. A sea captain needs a compass by which to steer or risks becoming lost in the vast ocean. That compass must work properly, its needle pointing to true north. Faulty information, if trusted, can lead to financial shipwreck. So it is with the choices that accompany getting older. The difference between getting lost and making it safely and securely to port has a great deal to do with the accuracy of the information we use to guide us.

CHAPTER TWO

The Retirement Advice Tsunami

"When your mother asks, 'Do you want a piece of advice?' it is a mere formality. It doesn't matter if you answer yes or no. You're going to get it anyway."

~ Erma Bombeck

I love that quote from Erma Bombeck about mothers giving advice. My mother and I were more like sisters growing up because she was still in her teens when I was born. But I know exactly where the famous humorist was coming from when she wrote those words that introduce this chapter. Motherly advice, or in a more expansive sense, *family advice* from those who love you, is something you are going to get whether you want to hear it or not. Where would we be in our lives had we not received some advice from those who loved us — and loved us enough to tell us what we **needed** to hear, not necessarily what we **wanted** to hear. I know I got a full dose of it from my grandmother and my older stepsisters growing up. I appreciate it now more than I did then.

I have always been a sponge for information, regardless of its source. That is a good thing, I believe. But in all honesty, I have to tell you that when it comes to advice on money, you have to be careful. There is just so much financial advice out there these days that it is overwhelming, even to a professional. I can only imagine what it must be like for a lay person to encounter a flood of contradictory and cross-directional advice when they turn the half-century corner. The airwaves are crowded with financial experts spewing forth differing opinions on what you should do with your hard-earned money. On the rare occasions when I watch the financial channels on cable TV, I shake my head in amazement to see grown people bickering in front of the camera like children on a playground. Producers of these programs like to keep us entertained with the point-counterpoint drama. Entertaining? Maybe. But such chatter does little to educate and inform us about how to plan for our financial future. Instead of calm, measured dialogue, we generally hear opponents and proponents of a particular stock debate with each other.

"Buy Apple now! It's a steal!"

"Run! Sell all your Apple shares now! The ship is going down!"

On one of the channels, a man comes on the set with his sleeves rolled up and his tie askew, wearing a party hat. Ostensibly, he is there to offer financial advice. But when a caller dials in with a question, he screams the answer and prances about the set ringing cow bells and squeezing bulb horns. The show is so bizarre that I just can't take anything he says seriously. He lost me at the cow bell. But it does get your attention. I confess, I've watched him rant for 10 minutes or so. I'm not sure it counts as "entertainment," though. It's the same fascination we have when we can't turn away from one of those gaudy reality shows. It might even be comedy if it weren't for the fact that some have lost large sums of money taking his advice.

He will occasionally get one of his stock picks right. When the stock takes off and does well, you hear about it in full stereo accompanied by sound effects. The effect that has is to inspire confidence in him as the mad genius stock market guru he purports to be. But when he is wrong (and he often is) there's nary a whisper of apology. One of the worst calls our boy with the bulb horn and the funny hat ever made was in 2008 just before the collapse of Bear Stearns, the "too big to fail" investment bank. He yelled tantrum-style at the camera, "Bear Stearns is fine! Bear Stearns is fine!" Bear Stearns, of course, wasn't fine. You never heard a peep from him on that one.

My point is this. Please understand this fare for what it is: entertainment, not financial counseling. It definitely isn't comedy. Just ask those who lost money on his predictions. They're not laughing.

Bad Investment Advice Is Everywhere

You know what I mean by "water cooler advice," don't you? You do if you have ever worked in an office and had a co-worker whisper to you about a ground floor opportunity. You are made to feel lucky indeed to be part of his or her inner circle of friends who are privy to this hot stock tip. Usually this well-meaning soul knows someone who has a friend who knows someone who has the inside track about this stock which is certain to be the next Google or Apple, and you have to act fast before the opportunity disappears. "Let's teach those Wall Street fat cats a lesson and beat them at their own game!" I think you know how this one ends.

What is it they say about free investment advice you hear at the water cooler? That it is usually worth exactly what you pay for it.

The Print Media

Recently I was in a book store looking for a book by Steven Covey, one of my favorite authors. When I passed by the magazine section, I was flabbergasted at (a) how many magazines are printed on every subject imaginable and (b) how many magazines were on the shelves that pertain to money. There were the old stand-bys with which I was familiar, like Kiplinger's, Money and Consumer Reports. But there were seemingly dozens of others that I had never heard of. And they all seemed to be competing for attention with sensational headlines like:

"Why GOLD Is a Smart Investment!"

"Don't Miss Out on the Petroleum Boom!"

If you scan the rack, you will inevitably find a headline or an article that advises you in the exact opposite direction.

Many of the headlines lure you in with promises of high returns:

"Get 8% Returns While the Getting is Good!"

"Put Your Lazy Money to Work Earning 10% Interest!"

Trouble is, when you read the article, every other line explains away the headline with disclaimers and attribution to a rare case that is likely never to be duplicated.

The thing that bothers me the most about these headlines is what is behind it all. Most of these magazines are merely advertising vehicles that contain little in the way of substance but prey on either greed or fear. People who have saved some money for their retirement fear running out of those resources prematurely. Those who may have lost a significant portion of their savings during the 2008 market crash are seeking ways to make it up. The facts are these (even though they would not make good headlines):

- **There is no quick, easy way to financial success.** Did someone say, "What about lottery winners?" Have you ever seen the statistics on how many of those lottery winners stay rich? Most, in fact, don't even stay lucky; their lives usually ruined by the psychological and social bugaboos that accompany their sudden, unearned wealth.

- **Get-rich-quick schemes are nearly always scams** that waste your resources. Does the name Bernie Madoff ring a bell? He was only able to pull off the greatest Ponzi scheme in history because people believed in something that was too good to be true.

- **No one knows the future.** Anyone who claims to know the future of the stock market is either an ill-intentioned liar or a well-meaning victim of delusion.

Friends and Family Advisors

I have to be very careful with what I'm about to say. I may be talking smack about your favorite Aunt Maddie, good old Uncle Fred or, God forbid, your children!

Because finding trustworthy advice is not always easy, and because some experienced financial professionals are perceived as being unreliable, motivated by profit or even dishonest, people naturally turn to those they feel they can trust — their family and friends. The problem is bad advice can come from good people. Family members can be great sounding boards. We know one thing; they are likely to have our best interests at heart. The problem is that our friends and family members are reluctant to utter the one phrase that I most admire from people who don't know what they are talking about: "I don't know."

Oops! Was that a little too straightforward? Unfortunately, it's true. I am sure that I can find relatives who would be willing to give me advice on everything from car repairs to major surgery. I know some friends who would be happy to weigh in with their opinion on virtually any problem that you could present to them. Why? Because they sincerely want to help. While that is a commendable sentiment, it still doesn't mean they know what they are talking about. I think sometimes even our closest friends, without realizing it, tend to project their own feelings and opinions onto us, even happy to have us make the same mistakes they make under the mistaken impression that somehow the shared misery will draw us closer.

When friends and relatives recommend a financial advisor, that's a good thing. Since many of the clients with whom I have enjoyed a professional relationship for now well over a decade have been referrals from others, I heartily support this practice for obvious reasons. But I would like to think that the referrals come with an explanation, not just, "Sandy is a great person to work with," or some other vague reason. If a friend or relative recommends a financial advisor to you, listen for that second sentence that tells you **why** you should follow their recommendation. "John is a great person to work with... **because** he helped me set up a lifetime income plan that covers all my basic expenses and was easy for me to understand."

Samples of Bad Financial Advice

While we are on the subject of bad financial advice and how to sift through it all, here is a sampling from the archives of some of the bad advice I have seen given, followed, and, more often than not, regretted.

"Why bother? – You don't have enough money to invest."

How ridiculous! If you are not heavily in debt and you have a six-month emergency fund then you can probably budget a small amount of money for savings. With today's technology, nearly everyone can start investing. Remember, large oaks start with small acorns. Save a little bit regularly each week in an account that yields compound interest and it will produce good results. Learning the discipline of a saver when young fosters healthy financial habits that can last a lifetime.

"You are too young to think about retirement."

No way! When you are young is exactly the time you *should* be thinking of your eventual retirement. The earlier you start saving, the better. If you have a 401(k) or similar tax-deferred retirement savings plan at your place of employment, contribute the maximum. If your employer offers a matching amount, take advantage of that, please!

I cannot tell you how many young people I give this lecture to when they tell me they don't participate in their company's retirement program, even when their employer offers to match their contributions. That is *free money*, people! Because retirement is decades away for some they find it hard to even visualize it. It's never too early to start saving for retirement.

"Buying a house is always a good investment."

Try telling that to someone who jumped into a mortgage shortly before the housing crisis hit in 2007 and subsequently found themselves on the wrong end of foreclosure proceedings. Buying a house can be a good investment, but you have to go into the transaction with your eyes wide open. Make sure you can afford the payments and that the decision is long-term. What got many in trouble during the housing crunch was assuming that the value of real estate would always escalate. Some bought multiple properties using exotic adjustable rate mortgages with the intention of reselling the properties to make a profit. That was a disaster for most of them. The real estate market has the potential for volatility just like the stock market. There are no guarantees. You have no idea where the market will be headed in two years' time.

Even if you can afford to buy the house, you should be able to make a down payment of 20 percent of the sale price. Don't forget other costs, such as property taxes, closing costs and insurance. If you are a first-time home buyer, owning a home puts you in a different league when it comes to expenses. Now you will have to pay for utilities and maintenance, which can cost a bundle.

"Go ahead and tap into your 401(k) if you need cash before retirement."

Please don't do that. View your 401(k) money as untouchable. Forget it's there. I have seen some people use their retirement account to pay for new cars, vacations, weddings and the like. It's like poking holes in the hot-air balloon you hope will carry you off to a carefree retirement someday. The essence of a 401(k) or similar retirement program is that you are deferring taxes. This allows a larger principle to continue to grow. As much as adding a regular contribution to that account propels that growth, taking premature withdrawals retards that growth. And there is the fact that you will pay a penalty on any amount withdrawn before age 59 ½. Not to mention that you will be paying income taxes on the money you withdraw or that you will miss out on the future compound growth potential of those withdrawals. The 401(k) is a powerful tool for retirement, but you must leave it alone.

That said, there are exceptions. The IRS does recognize certain circumstances such as avoiding foreclosure, medical expenses and other provable hardships. But for the most part, just pretend that money isn't there until you retire and you will be much better off.

"Go ahead and spend it while you got it. You only go around once."

I'm not saying that you shouldn't give yourselves a treat now and then when you are young. Go ahead and blow a hundred dollars on something frivolous like a weekend getaway or some digital something or other you want but don't really need. But save up for it and use what you allocated and no more. Bad advice like this usually comes from someone who doesn't appreciate the value of saving and has no budget. My father used to say, "Never spend the grocery money on the movies." In other words, pay your bills first before you play. Never spend more than you know you can afford. And whatever you do, don't use a credit card to satisfy a whim just because that's what your friends are doing.

When Financial Advisors Don't Agree

It's no wonder some people throw up their hands in frustration over financial planning when they have so many pundits offering conflicting advice.

"Put all your money in the market."

"The market is too risky."

"The 4 percent rule works."

"No it doesn't."

"Annuities are great."

"Annuities are terrible."

I could go on and on. Sometimes when I see the talking heads go at it on TV with their conflicting opinions, it reminds me of two rams butting heads on nature documentaries.

It shouldn't surprise us that professionals differ in their approach on some issues. Take the medical field for example. I have a friend who once told me that he suffered from back pain. He went to several doctors, seeking help.

The neurologist told him that he needed an MRI and probably surgery to correct a bulging disc. The doctor prescribed anti-inflammatory medication and muscle relaxers to relieve the immediate pain.

A chiropractor recommended that he come in for regular treatments on the adjustment table and prescribed stretching exercises.

An alternative medical practitioner suggested acupuncture.

A lumbar specialist said that surgery wasn't necessary and derided the idea of chiropractic treatment and acupuncture as voodoo. The lumbar specialist recommended a specially fitted back brace and then possible surgery — but only after a year if the brace didn't help.

In the end, my friend's back did get better. He took the muscle relaxers and the pain pills, made regular visits to the chiropractor, did the stretches and wore the back brace. He also lost 25 pounds. He says that to this day he doesn't know what made his back pain go away; he is just happy it did.

So, which doctor was right? Perhaps all of them were right, to a degree, anyway. The reason why those duly licensed, fully accredited medical professionals disagreed with each other on how to treat back pain was because of the training they had each received. Different schools and different schools of thought.

It's the same in the professional advisory community. There are those who only know one way to approach a problem — the stock market. It's how they were indoctrinated by the big brokerages they represent. Then there are those who know only the insurance industry side of the financial advisory business. It's what they learned when they first obtained their insurance license and they likely never bothered to become securities licensed. So their solutions to retirement planning will always be an insurance product, such as life insurance or annuities. There is an old saying: "To someone who only has a hammer, every problem looks like a nail."

Have you ever noticed that the truth is usually somewhere in the middle? That is certainly the case when it comes to financial planning. It's like a tailored suit — designed for no one but you. It may include a product from this school of thought, a strategy from that financial discipline and an income planning technique from somewhere else. An effective retirement plan is usually a combination of concepts and strategies that all work together to achieve a single, precise goal.

When it comes to financial advice, don't be afraid to trust yourself. You may not be a financial advisor, but it is your money. It's your retirement. It's your future. Don't be afraid to trust your instincts when you come across something that just doesn't sound right or add up. There is no one-size-fits-all when it comes to financial plans. They are as individual as fingerprints and have to be tailor-made to your unique and individual circumstances.

I can't imagine intentionally buying a pair of shoes that don't fit.

"Size eight please"

"Try these. They're size seven, but they're really well made and I think they will look good on you."

"No. I wear size eight."

"How about these? They are size 10, but they are really well made and we are running a special... today only."

Are you walking out of that shoe store? Me too!

My Advice on Advice

- If you feel pressured to sign or buy anything, walk away.
- Beware of anything that sounds too good to be true. It probably is.
- If advice doesn't ring true, or can't be validated by your own independent research, there is usually a reason. Follow the money trail.
- It's OK to ask financial professionals how they are remunerated. Everyone gets paid for their work in America, so there's nothing wrong with that. But financial advisors should always put your interests ahead of their own. You can usually sense it when they do. And you can usually sense it if they don't.
- If you are in a Ford dealership, don't expect them to brag about Chevrolets.
- A true professional will solve problems, not sell products.
- A true professional will ask lots of questions and answer all of yours readily and in full detail.
- At the end of the day, the best advice is the kind you give yourself after you acquire a comprehensive education about the issues at hand. Become more knowledgeable about retirement and the planning that goes with it. The time you spend learning about finance, investments and other matters pertaining to how best to handle your wealth can result in huge benefits.

CHAPTER THREE

Saving, Investing and Debt When You're Young

"Having more money doesn't make you happier. I have 50 million dollars but I'm just as happy as when I had 48 million."

~ Arnold Schwarzenegger.

I began learning about money and the meaning of money at age 4. My parents owned and operated a meat-packing plant in Wickliffe, Kentucky, right at the point where the Ohio and Mississippi rivers meet. My mother ran the office and took me to work with her. To alleviate my boredom, she gave me a box of crayons and allowed me to draw and color on the white butcher paper that she would tear off large rolls. One day a very nice customer came over to admire my work and offered to buy my childish masterpiece for a quarter. Instantly, I was an entrepreneur!

From then on I would ask waiting customers if they would like to have one of my original works of art. They were only 35 cents (the law of supply and demand at work). Sometimes I would be offered as much as a dollar or more for my "portraits." No, they weren't very good, but I was just a little kid. I coasted on the "cute factor" as long as it lasted. I quickly learned about sales, too. If I wanted to "move the merchandise," I couldn't wait for them to notice me… I had to approach them.

I remember coming to some conclusions about money at that tender age — financial truths if you will — that to this day still serve as a cornerstone to financial success. Along with the possession of money came the decision as to what to do with it. I had choices to make and sub-choices under those choices. I could (a) spend the money. If I spent the money, what would I spend on? I could also (b) save the money. If I chose to save the money, to what use would I put it? Money is only so much metal and paper unless you have a goal in mind, I realized. But it gave me a good feeling to count it and watch it grow. I received a sense of satisfaction in the acquisition and possession of my little stash. I became an investor, too. When my crayons became nubs, I bought a new and bigger box of crayons. By the time I was 6 years old, I had saved enough to buy my very own swing set.

As I got older and the "cute factor" began to fade, I did what many businesses have to do to survive — I restructured. I learned how to crochet. I discovered that I could take ordinary hand towels, cut them in half, crochet the tops with fancy designs and sell them for a handsome profit. They were useful and decorative. I could not keep them in stock at Christmas time. By the time I entered middle school I had added to my sales force. My grandmother worked at a foam rubber factory and would take my products to work with her and sell them there. I also had a marketing program. One towel sold for $3.00 and a matching set of two sold for $5.00. The very important lessons that I learned as a young girl about money were these:

- You tend to place a greater value on money you have to work for as opposed to money that is given to you.
- The acquisition of money brings with it decisions and choices.
- Money can be either spent or saved. Spending it brings temporary enjoyment but saving it brings you a deeper satisfaction and a feeling of self-worth.

- You can either have money, or you can have what money will buy, but you can't have both. Once you spend it, money is gone.

Those simple truths carry over into adult life. What occurred to me at the age of 4 — that industry can create wealth but only discipline can preserve it — is a core belief that I apply to myself and my clients to this very day.

The Difference Between Saving and Investing

Saving money is putting it away. Investing money is putting it to work for you. To illustrate, squirrels save nuts in the fall. Growing up in Kentucky my favorite season was autumn when the leaves would put on a color show that lasted for about two weeks in late October and early November. Have you ever watched squirrels in the fall? They seem to be the busiest of creatures, dashing urgently from limb to limb, scurrying along the ground, gathering food for the winter. Instinct tells them to scramble around collecting nuts, seeds and other edibles and place them in various hiding places so that when cold weather comes they will have something to eat.

Biologists tell us that squirrels hoard these morsels in several different locations, not just one tree. When you see squirrels in that sitting position and they look like they are munching at something in their little paws, they are actually leaving their scent on the food so they can locate and retrieve it later.

Savings are like those hoards of nuts. The acorns don't multiply in the hollow of the tree; they merely sit there for later use. Most people associate savings with the bank — savings accounts, checking accounts and certificates of deposit. Those accounts don't pay much in the way of interest and you don't expect them to. You do want them to be safe. These accounts are insured by the Federal Deposit Insurance Corporation (FDIC). And they are liquid. Savings and checking accounts can be accessed immediately and often from remote locations. The tradeoff for this security and ready availability is that your money isn't really working for you.

Investing, on the other hand, is more like farming. You plant your seeds at the most favorable time of the season for growth potential. You hope the weather cooperates and you expect to reap more than what you sowed. Farming is risky business sometimes. Just ask a farmer who has experienced drought, a flood or a freeze during the growing season. You hope for a bumper crop, but you could have crop failure.

When you invest, you have a greater chance of losing your money than when you save. Unlike FDIC-insured deposits, the money you invest in securities, mutual funds and other similar investments is not federally insured. You could lose your "principal," which is the initial amount you invested. That's true even if you purchase your investments through a bank. But when you invest, you also have the opportunity to earn more money than when you save. There is a tradeoff between the higher risk of investing and the potential for greater rewards.

The Miracle of Compound Interest

I was never really **taught** the value of money... I learned it by myself. It puzzles me why the principles of budgeting, savings and investing are not taught in our public schools. I am not aware of any courses being taught in high schools on how to handle one's personal finances. I don't recall seeing any curriculum when I attended school that included instructions on how to balance a checkbook. I learned nothing in high school about compound interest, tax-deferred retirement accounts, life insurance, annuities or how the stock market functions. To the best of my knowledge it was the same when my son was in school and it is the same with the education my grandson, who is in elementary school as this is written, is receiving.

Am I missing something here? Shouldn't this type of real-world training be offered to our children? I think I will put it on my to-do list to one day write a children's book entitled *"Dick and Jane Learn to Save*

Money" and campaign for it to be included in the libraries of all elementary schools.

For high schoolers, I will have to develop a book that somehow explains how the stock market works, or some other feature of the world economy, but build it around a vampire theme. I've got it! I will entitle it *"Twilight Investors in Love."* Maybe then the kids would read it. They tend to read books if the word "Twilight" is in the title, right?

But seriously, if students are not taught such simple principles as saving for retirement, how to invest or how to avoid the trap of consumer credit card debt, we are leaving them to fend for themselves. As a result of this omission many young people enter the real world without a clue as to how to manage money. It's a little like putting them behind the wheel of a car without driver's training. Education on how to drive a car is a base the schools seem to cover pretty well. Education on how to manage money, save for the future and invest it wisely... not so much.

Most young people don't need any lessons on how to spend money. That seems to come instinctually. The concept of saving is what we need to teach them. For the sake of motivation, let's start at the end — the **reason why** young people should save at least 10 percent of the money they accumulate.

The Eighth Wonder of the World

Because he was a genius, many people attribute quotations to Albert Einstein that if he were alive today he would scratch his bushy head and say, "I don't remember saying that." One of those quotes is: "Compound interest is the eighth wonder of the world." Whether or not he said it does not take anything away from the miracle of compound interest when it comes to saving money. Compound interest can turn a little bit of money into a whole lot of money, given enough time. Time is the greatest ally of young savers. In fact, the more time you have on your side, the more miraculous compound interest becomes.

Here's the way it works: when you invest or save money, it earns interest. Let's say you place a sum of money into an account. The next year, assuming you don't touch it, you earn interest on the original sum *plus interest on the interest.* In the third year, you earn interest on the original sum *plus interest on the first two years,* and so forth and so on. Earning interest on interest and then earning more interest on that interest can be likened to a snowball rolling downhill. It starts slow and small but builds upon itself until, depending on how far it rolls, it grows to the size of a boulder. If the interest is like the accumulating snow, the hill can be likened to time. If you started rolling your snowball from the top of the hill and someone else started rolling their snowball in the middle of the hill, yours would naturally be much greater in size. The earlier you start saving and investing, the more money you have at the end of the trail.

You probably learned the story of Christopher Columbus in elementary school — how that in 1492 he "sailed the ocean blue" to discover the new world. Imagine that Columbus found a penny on his way to visit Queen Isabella. And let's say that, instead of putting that penny in his pocket or spending it, he put that penny in an account earning 6 percent interest. Let also say that he then selected someone whom he could trust to carry out his instructions and told them to leave the penny there, but remove the interest every year and put that interest in a piggy bank. Between then and now, the total value of the contents of that piggy bank would be an unimpressive 30 cents.

But if Columbus had placed that penny in an account returning 6 percent interest, and if he had allowed the interest to compound for all these centuries, the account would be worth (drum roll please)... more than $121 billion dollars today!

I don't blame you if you want to check the math. I did. I came across this illustration in 2009 and the instructions to check the math were as follows: Multiply .01 times 1.06 percent, and repeat 517 times (or the number of years since 1492). If you could tap the key 517 times without losing count, you should come up with 121,096,709,346.21, assuming your calculator can count that high.

Can you see now why Albert Einstein, if the attribution is true, was so impressed with compound interest? Now, granted, you are unlikely to live 517 years to collect on a one-cent investment, but it makes the point, doesn't it, that saving small amounts when you're young enables you to have a boatload of money later on?

For a more practical example, consider the case of Jane, age 22, who starts working after college and is able to save $300 per month into an account earning 10 percent compound interest. By age 28, she decides to quit working and raise a family. She stops contributing the $300 per month, but she just leaves the money alone and lets it grow. If Jane never contributed another penny to the account, she would have an account worth over $1 million by the time she turns 65.

Remember the snowball that started rolling downhill in the middle of the hill? That's Tom. He is one of those people who postponed saving money until he was 31. Can he still be a millionaire by the time he retires? Yes, but it will be tougher. In order for him to get there, he would have to kick in the same $300 per month for the next 34 years to earn $1 million by the time he turns 65. Total amount contributed by Tom: $126,000 over 34 years. Why the big difference? Jane's money had more time to grow at compound interest.

Interest Works Both Ways

Interest works both ways, you know. You pay it when you borrow and you earn it when you save or invest. Debt can turn compound interest from a wonderful blessing into an ugly curse. If you have a revolving charge account, your debt can approach 25 percent or more! Debt sneaks up on you when you're young. After all, you are the perfect target for the free enterprise system. You are active. You are discovering the world. It's like the horn of plenty is putting all of this stuff in front of you and you want to use it, wear it, drive it or in some other way consume it. Merchants, to make it easy for you to fulfill your desires with offers to buy now and pay later, came up with a plan.

Children today do not know what it was like to live in a world without personal computers, smartphones, scanners or fax machines. It is polite of these young people not to point out how we older people cling to some of our anachronisms. Have you ever noticed on a computer that little icon you click to save a document? It's represents the obsolete 3 ½ inch floppy disk. We don't even use those anymore, but it lives on as the icon for "save this file." Have you ever *dialed* a wrong number on a touch-tone phone? Talk about your carry-over from days gone by, how about raised numbers on credit cards? When is the last time you have had a cashier use the manual slide roller to record a credit card transaction? Don't they scan everything with a magnetic strip now? You know you are over 50 if you know what an eight-track tape was. I still say "tape" when I want to record. Old habits die hard.

Dollar Cost Averaging

Young savers have no better friend than dollar cost averaging. Because time is on your side, young reader, you can build a tidy sum for retirement by simply saving consistently and leaving it alone. Here's what I mean. Do you have a 401(k) plan at work? And does your employer match a portion of what you contribute to it? If the answer is yes, please tell me that you contribute the maximum to it. Especially if you have an employer match. That's *free money!*

I know some young people who blink and stare into space when I ask them about their *tax-deferred, qualified, defined-contribution savings plan,* otherwise known as a 401(k) or perhaps 403(b). Both are retirement savings programs named after paragraphs in the IRS code that spell out their provisions. The main advantage to these plans is that they allow you to save money for the future without paying taxes on either the money you contribute or the amount of interest they earn until you withdraw it years later.

Here's what I mean by dollar cost averaging. When you send a portion of your paycheck to your 401(k) plan do you know where it goes? Typically it goes to the plan's custodian, such as Fidelity or Vanguard. They take that money and buy as many shares of XYZ mutual fund as possible. If the share price goes up, no problem — your account just went up in value. If the share price of XYZ mutual fund goes down, congratulations! You just bought more shares. Don't worry, those skinny shares will fatten up eventually because *time is on your side,* remember? Either way, you can't lose if you are consistent with your contributions and you leave the account alone until you are ready to retire.

Just as dollar cost averaging is a young saver's best friend, **reverse** dollar cost averaging is a retiree's worst enemy. Let's say you have been contributing to your 401(k) for decades. Then you retire. You no longer receive a paycheck. You no longer contribute to your retirement program; it is now time for your retirement program to contribute to your retirement. You will be writing a check to yourself, say, each month to meet your expenses. *If you don't move your 401(k)* to a position of safety, away from market risk, instead of **buying** shares with each **contribution,** you will be **selling** shares with each **withdrawal.** You are now probably in a situation where you have to withdraw the same amount each month, regardless of the share price. If shares of XYZ mutual fund are up, you sell fewer of them to withdraw that amount. If shares of XYZ mutual fund are down, you sell more shares to withdraw that same amount. Either way, you are depleting your account. Time that was on your side when you were building the account is no longer on your side. A downturn in the market could wipe out your savings pretty quickly, and there's nothing you can do about it.

That's why prudent retirees move the money they need to live on in retirement away from market risk once they near the retirement zone.

Debt Can Be a Killer

This may be easy to say and hard to do, but, other than perhaps your home mortgage and maybe your automobiles, there is no good reason to go into personal debt. If I'm your financial advisor, I'm going to encourage you to pay cash for everything you buy and avoid consumer debt, especially credit card debt, like the plague.

Remember the penny Christopher Columbus found. Every little spoonful you can cram into a savings account now will come back to you in buckets when you retire. To help you accomplish that, please consider some of the following. I call them "saver skillsets." The more of them you master, the more wealth you can accumulate for your eventual retirement.

Live within your means. First you have to know what your "means" are. How much money do you earn? What are your necessary expenses, such as food, clothing, shelter, and transportation? If you put those two things down in two separate columns, you have just created a rudimentary budget. Now it is simple (perhaps not easy, but simple). Don't spend more than you make. What's that old saying: "If your outgo exceeds your income then your upkeep will be your downfall?" Something like that.

Once you have established your budget, you can find places to tweak it to achieve your goals. By tweaking, I mean you can spend less or earn more, not spend more than you earn. I remember as a kid growing up that we had everything we *needed,* but we didn't always get everything we *wanted.* As long as my father was around, we never had any problem confusing the two things. Do you *need* a new car? Or do you just *want* a new car?

There's an old saying that goes: "You can't have your cake and eat it too." Translated for our purposes, that means that you can either have the money that it takes to buy something or you can have the money itself, but you can't have both. When you are tempted to use the plastic to purchase something you want but do not need, ask yourself, "Do I really want to pay interest on a suede jacket? Or a new pair of designer jeans?" The little angel on your right shoulder tells you to put them back on the shelf and walk away. But as your hand moves toward the shelf, that little red devil on your left shoulder whispers in your ear: "Hey, jeans are clothing...clothing is a *need.*" That's the little game we play with ourselves, isn't it? But inside, we know the truth, don't we?

Free Advice to Young People

I know you haven't hired me as your financial advisor yet, but you did buy my book, so, with your permission, I will take the liberty to offer some free advice that I hope you will find useful and profitable.

Take charge of your own financial future. Everyone is eager to advise you when you are young. Nothing elicits human good nature more than someone who is lost and needs directions. If you don't believe this, just stop your car, lower your window and ask someone where the nearest interstate is. No matter what their disposition is under ordinary circumstances, they will turn nice and try to help you... even the ones who don't have a clue as to where the interstate is! You will also get advice from well-meaning souls about managing your finances, even when they know very little about the subject. It could be your neighbor who knows somebody who has a cousin in Chicago who gave him a tip on a stock that can't lose. Or it could be your Aunt Mildred who really wants you to buy a house, even though you can only afford one of those treacherous adjustable-rate mortgages. It is crucial that you take charge of managing your financial future or someone else will attempt to manage, or in some cases mismanage, it for you.

Are there any unscrupulous people who call themselves financial professionals? Ever heard of Bernie Madoff? Then there are those well-meaning folks who can run your financial ship aground, just because they don't know what they are doing. I invite you to take charge of your financial future by reading books on personal finance. Know how much you are spending, saving and earning. Know where you have your savings and why you have it there. Ask questions of your banker, or whoever represents the custodian in whose hands you have placed your "rainy day money." When you get financial statements, open them, read them and, if you don't understand them, ask questions until you do.

Save it now and spend it later. I saw a clever cartoon the other day. Two neighbors were talking over a fence. The name on the mailbox was "Jones," which tipped you off to the fact that the neighbor who was speaking was named Jones (clever cartoonist). So Jones says to his neighbor, *"I'm sorry to hear that you were keeping up with us... we just declared bankruptcy."* I guess the moral of the story is, don't let yourself become unduly influenced by your friends, or neighbors in this case, to spend beyond your means. Just because your friend is driving a new four-wheel drive SUV shouldn't move you to buy one too if you can't afford it. If your friends fly to the Greek Islands for a scenic cruise and you can't afford to go along, say "no" graciously but firmly. Remember your savings goals. If you are faithful to your savings program, you will be able to buy your own island one day. If your desire to pay off your credit card is greater than your desire to go clubbing, you won't go clubbing just because your friends are doing it. Let your friends in on why you are turning down their invitations so they'll know it's not personal, it's financial.

Pinch pennies; they make dollars later on. Within reason, cut costs whenever possible. Buy things when they're on sale. Clip coupons. Eat before you go to the movies instead of "investing" in popcorn, candy and drinks. Come to think about it, wait until the movie comes out on DVD and rent it from the dollar vending machine around the corner! Eat before you go to a restaurant and then order an appetizer. Have fun, but make a supreme effort to stick to your budget and your savings program without being too weird. Keep thinking of that penny Columbus found.

Develop good spending/saving habits. If you want to create a new habit, whether it's eating a piece of fruit for lunch, getting more exercise or posting your blog every day, behavior experts say it takes 21 days to form a new habit. Once you are in a habit of consulting your budget before spending money frivolously, you will do it automatically, even if you do the math in your head. It's the same with savings. Chunk that money into your savings account every paycheck until it becomes your financial heartbeat. Years from now, somewhere on a sandy beach without a care in the world, your older self will offer a toast to your younger self and sincerely thank you.

CHAPTER FOUR

Shifting Gears: Moving From Accumulation to Distribution

"Wood burns faster when you have to cut and chop it yourself."

~ Harrison Ford

People who know me now probably wouldn't believe what I was like in school as a child. I was a shy kid with not many friends. I had red hair and freckles and I wore braces, if that gives you a mental picture. In those early years I had a reading and comprehension challenge, too. I received very little help at home, so I struggled a lot. Fortunately I had some great teachers and found a great friend in a girl named Jennifer Jones. We hit it off right away for some reason. We had disparate backgrounds. Her parents owned a truck stop and had money. My family got by somehow. She had a small electric car her parents had given her. One of my most fond memories is going up and down her very long driveway, waving at invisible crowds on her spacious lawn, pretending we were beauty queens.

What's that got to do with retirement you ask? We all go through phases in our lives. As I said, I'm not that timid little girl anymore. I metamorphosed. One of my favorite poems is "The Chambered Nautilus," by Oliver Wendell Holmes. He wrote:

> *"Build thee more stately mansions, O my soul,*
> *As the swift seasons roll!*
> *Leave thy low-vaulted past!*
> *Let each new temple, nobler than the last..."*

The chambered nautilus is a sea creature that lives in a spiral-shaped shell that is divided into successively larger compartments, or "chambers," as the mollusk outgrows them throughout its life.

In our early years, way before we hit the big "five-O," we are in the ***accumulation*** financial phase of our life. We are chunking away our savings and allowing our money to grow through investing (hopefully) until we have enough of a stash to help us retire in relative comfort. We go through phases during the accumulation years, too. Typically we start out solo. We join the work force when we are single. Most successful people I know took the first job that came along when they were teenagers just to get started. It didn't matter if it was flipping burgers or washing cars. We just wanted to work and get paid. My first job was at the Jiffy Mart in Wickliffe, Kentucky, for a measly $87 per week. I didn't care. It was a way to join the adult working world.

Our next phase during accumulation may be building a family. Like the chambered nautilus, we need larger living spaces as our families grow.

The ***preservation*** phase of life starts when retirement comes into view. We aren't there yet, we have a few more years to go, but we are approaching it. It's like driving out West on those long straight highways of the Great Plains headed toward the mountains. You see the mountain as a blue haze on the horizon at first and then it gets larger in the windshield until it takes on definition. You can't even see retirement when you are in those early accumulation years. Not really. It's so far off that it may as well not be there. Then when you turn the bend of age 50, it appears in your field of vision and takes on definition. More details about your life appear. You are more careful with your investing. When

they turn 50, get what I call "deer in the headlights" syndrome. They can't decide what to do so they don't do anything — that is until the deadline for taking some action or another forces them to make a decision in a hurry; sometimes they make the wrong one.

We used to encounter whitetail deer on the secondary roads of rural Kentucky where I grew up and it was true that they would sometimes freeze in the high-beam headlights of approaching cars. Becoming immobile in the face of imminent danger is, well, dangerous!

People can be that way when it comes to some of the decisions they must make when they approach retirement. Many of the decisions having to do with setting up our retirement will involve government programs, such as Medicare and Social Security. They will come with a degree of complexity. Some folks, because they want to make the right choices but are confused by that complexity, get frustrated and dome down with "indecision-itis." They freeze in the headlights just like those deer.

This is just one more reason to get some help. Seek the advice of a skilled professional who specializes in these areas and knows how to lay out your options for you so they make sense. We can arrive at many retirement decisions by process of elimination, once we understand our options clearly. Postponing them until the last minute is unnecessary. We would not postpone medical treatment simply because it is complex. If surgical skills were easy to master, medical schools would require only six months' training instead of eight years. When faced with complex financial decisions, by all means have your options explained to you by a professional and get a second opinion and even a third if you don't fully understand.

When You Need a Specialist

When you were young, you probably saw a pediatrician for medical treatment. But once you moved beyond those years and became an adult, you needed doctors with a different kind of training. The same is true of financial advice. When you are young and in the accumulation phase your financial advisor should specialize in accumulation. When you turn 50, however, it's an entirely different financial landscape. Accumulation of assets may be job one when you are in your 30s and 40s, but when you round the half-century mark, preservation of assets becomes critical.

The financial advisor who got you *to* retirement is usually not the one to get you *through* retirement.

"But we're friends!" Some people say that about their current financial advisor — the one who got them to retirement. In that case you may have yet one more decision to give some thought to and make accordingly. Which is more important to you? The relationship, or knowing where to place your steps as you cross what is increasingly the confusing and treacherous turf of retirement.

In the medical community, it's considered a professional courtesy among doctors to refer patients to a specialist when they need it. Not so much in the financial world. It may be because retirement planning and accumulation are such different worlds. Whatever the reason, it is incumbent on each investor to ask the right questions of the advisor candidate to make sure he or she is getting the right advice. More on that later.

CHAPTER FIVE

Rethinking the Three-Legged Retirement Stool

"We will keep the promise of Social Security by taking the responsible steps to strengthen it — not by turning it over to Wall Street."

~ Barack Obama

There was a time when financial people referred to retirement as a three-legged stool. The three metaphorical legs were:

* Employer pension
* Personal savings
* Social Security

The idea was that when you retired, no one leg would get you through retirement comfortably, but with all three of them you had a tripod of support that could in all likelihood allow you to carry on the same lifestyle after your working years as you did before.

So what happened?

Well, for one thing, if pensions aren't extinct, they certainly are on the endangered list. Times were when the American worker could look forward to spending 30 or 40 years with the same company and be rewarded with a gold watch and a guaranteed lifetime paycheck. The pension payout may not be as much as the salary when working, but it did comprise one solid leg of the three-legged stool.

The demise of the defined benefit pension plan began after World War II with the Studebaker Corporation. For readers under age 30, Studebaker was a fancy automobile of the 1950s before tail fins came along. They were ahead of their time in many ways. Studebaker models had exciting names like "Avanti," "Lark" and "Speedster." Like Ford, Studebaker was named after its creator. John M. Studebaker started out making horse-drawn wagons in 1902. By the 1950s, Studebakers were known for their futuristic looks and aerodynamic design. One of the first new American cars to debut after the end of WWII was the 1947 Studebaker Champion Starlight coupe, which featured a few firsts — a wrap-around rear windshield and similar styling on both the front and the rear of the car. This novel design caused people to joke that you couldn't tell whether it was coming or going.

So what's all that got to do with pensions? For some reason, Americans just didn't go for the new look. Not even the powerful, sleek Avanti sports car could keep the auto maker from falling way behind Ford, General Motors and Chrysler. The venerable old company declared bankruptcy in the mid-1960s.

The unionized auto workers who built Studebakers had pretty good pension plans, thanks to the UAW (United Auto Workers). But when the laid-off workers started to claim them, they received a bit of a shock. Because of years of slumping sales, the pension plans had become poorly funded by the corporation. It was soon apparent that Studebaker couldn't keep its pension promises. Thousands of workers were informed that their payouts would be reduced. Thousands more were told that they would receive nothing at all. The workers were understandably upset. After all, they had worked all those years thinking they had a guaranteed income. Through the UAW, they complained loudly to Congress, which, in 1974, passed the Employee Retirement Income Security Act (ERISA). The new law purported to regulate pension plans, but the effect it had was to spell their doom.

One by-product of ERISA was a new law that allowed taxpayers to contribute as much as $1,500 (now $5,500) per year into something called an "individual retirement account," or, as you may know it better, the IRA.

This was history in the making. Millions of Americans still viewed the pension as the keystone of retirement. But with the combination of government regulation and tax incentives for personal savings, companies began shifting the obligation of caring for retiring workers away from the corporations and back to the individual workers and the government. By law, these new IRA accounts were allowed to actually **grow** tax deferred — which meant that workers would not have to pay taxes on their money until they withdrew it. This new law allowing individuals to reduce their taxable income by the amount contributed to an IRA was a boon to self-employed individuals who had no pension. IRA accounts began popping up like spring flowers around tax time when accountants informed their clients that they could reduce their taxes by simply opening up a tax-deferred account.

Some people wondered if Uncle Sam had lost his mind or was turning into Santa Claus. But the government wasn't giving away anything. The IRS knew exactly what it was doing. IRA accounts are not tax-free, they are merely tax-deferred. At some point, after the account has been allowed to grow, the tax man will collect his due, only this time from a much larger account. No, Uncle Sam wasn't crazy, just patient. Let's not forget, too, that he can print money when he needs it.

The 401(k) Arrives!

Just about everyone knows that a 401(k) is a type of defined contribution retirement plan established and maintained by employers for the benefit of employees. Not so many know why it sounds like a breakfast cereal. The name comes from section 401 of the IRS code, subsection K. The provision within the IRS code that made 401(k) plans possible was enacted into law in 1978. It was intended to give taxpayers a break on taxes and allow them save for retirement. The little paragraph apparently went unnoticed, or at least the potential provisions of it did, until 1980 when a benefits consultant named Ted Benna figured out that it could be used to create a simple, tax-advantaged way to save for retirement.

Essentially, 401(k)s put employees in charge of their own pension plan. The employer, instead of guaranteeing a payout, gets a tax break by contributing to the employee's plan. Not all employers do this, but when they do it is called "matching funds," since the employer matches a portion of the employee's contribution.

The first 401(k) plan began in 1981. There was little enthusiasm for them among employers at first, but the idea gained momentum in the bull markets of the 1990s. Now they have all but replaced defined benefit pension plans. As this is written, 401(k) plans contain more than $3.5 trillion in assets invested in them.

What are the pros and cons to the 401(k)? A pro is that these plans put the employee in charge of his own retirement savings/investment account. A negative is that, unlike the old pensions they replaced, 401(k) plans are not guaranteed. Typically, your contributions are deducted from your paycheck. They go to a fund manager, or custodian, such as Vanguard or Fidelity. The custodian uses the contribution to buy shares of mutual funds. Employees generally have some say in how the funds are invested, but it is usually according to a formula based on risk tolerance. You may, for example, elect to have 30 percent in small cap mutual funds, 20 percent in large cap mutual funds, 10 percent in international stocks and 40 percent in growth funds. But the actual buying of the shares is done by the fund managers. When the market goes up, your account value increases. When it goes down, so does the value of your account.

As pointed out, it's hard to get hurt if you are a young investor. But if you are approaching retirement, you could lose a sizable portion of your life's savings with a sudden market drop.

While we are on the subject, if you have a 401(k) and your employer offers to match a portion of it, by all means take the company up on that deal. Some employers match up to 6 percent of what you save. That's like free money.

The point is, whether you have a 401(k), 403(b) or SEP (simplified employee pension) plan because you are self-employed, or if you keep cash in a safe, that is one leg of the stool — your personal savings.

What to Do With a 401(k) When You Retire

When you retire, you have some decisions to make about your 401(k). Do you leave it with your former employer? Do you cash it out? Do you roll it over into an IRA?

Cashing out your 401(k) is a bad idea for several reasons. First of all, you will create a potentially huge tax event if you do that. The IRS will require that you pay income taxes at your current marginal tax rate on any lump sum you withdraw. Secondly, if you are younger than 59 ½, you will pay a 10 percent penalty. It's better to stretch out your distributions over many years to minimize the tax bite. Plus, delaying withdrawals as long as possible allows your money to continue to grow.

You have administrative fees associated with your 401(k) plan that can cut into your investment over the years. If you choose to roll over your money to an IRA, you may be able to avoid those fees, especially if you don't sign up for investment management at a brokerage. Once you are no longer an employee, some 401(k) plans charge an extra maintenance fee. Consult your company's plan administrator representative to see what the case is with your plan.

Changes can occur with your 401(k) at any time. The plan's trustees can change. Fees can change. You might not be aware of these changes as soon as they happen if you no longer work there, and you might not be able to react to them quickly. Usually, when significant changes to the retirement plan happen, the employer communicates these changes to employees by means of informational meetings. You will miss those if you have left the firm. Your only way of knowing how your account is being affected will be to view your account statements.

More control. Most 401(k) plans have restrictions. For example, some employers have a menu of investments that are available and allow no exceptions. Some require that the employer match be invested in company stock. Once you leave the employ of that company you may no longer be willing to accept those restrictions. You may prefer total control of your investments, especially if you are retired.

Fewer investment choices exist when your 401(k) is housed with your old employer than if you control it directly. Most of the funds company 401(k) plans are in have high expense ratios and high fees. When you roll over your money into an IRA you can invest in anything you want, including individual stocks or ETFs (exchange-traded funds) if you wish.

Employer stock — Some workers leave their 401(k)s parked with their former employers with a large portion of those assets invested in the former employer's stock. This is not a good idea. Anyone who remembers the Enron scandal knows the danger that lies here. Your ex-employer could go bankrupt or fall apart in any number of ways and there goes your retirement.

Orphan accounts are 401(k) type accounts left behind by workers who change jobs often and fail to roll over their retirement accounts to the new employer or to an IRA. I recommend you consolidate these accounts so you can more easily check on your investments. You may be pleasantly surprised at how much less you are paying in fees.

Bottom line? There are many things to deal with when you leave your job or career, but don't forget about your retirement account. This could be your largest investment if you worked with one employer for a long time.

Unless you are one of the lucky few who has a defined benefit pension plan, the only other viable leg of our erstwhile three-legged stool is Social Security. What do we know and what do we just think we know about this program?

CHAPTER SIX

Social Security – An American Treasure

"While it is clear that we need to make some adjustments to protect Social Security for the long term, it is disingenuous to say that the trust fund is facing a crisis."

~ Carl Levin

When President Franklin Roosevelt signed the Social Security Act on Aug. 14, 1935, he probably had no idea that eight decades later it would be such a popular program. These days, if you are running for public office, you dare not even hint that you will alter existing Social Security provisions and benefits. If you even comment on the future of the program, you must tread lightly lest your comments are misunderstood by the senior citizenry. Social Security remains one of the nation's most successful, effective and popular programs. Is it enough to live on for most retirees? No. But it provides a foundation of income on which workers can build to plan for their retirement. It also provides valuable social insurance protection to workers who become disabled and to families whose breadwinner dies. When you stop to think about it, with pensions disappearing, Social Security is one of the few incomes that are guaranteed for one's lifetime.

Setting up Your Social Security Account

I encourage people to go to the Social Security Administration website, www.socialsecurity.gov/myaccount, and set up their account so they can see what their projected income will be. It is sometimes eye-opening and the information helps you in making decisions regarding your retirement. It used to be that an annual benefits estimate would come to you in the mail three months before your birthday. Now the SSA saves about $70 million in printing and mailing costs by simply sending out an email asking people with an account to just view and verify your information. But first you have to set up the account. I didn't find it difficult and most of my clients tell me it was relatively easy to do. You will have to plug in such information as your Social Security number, date of birth, mailing address and email address. Anyone 18 years of age or older is allowed to set up an account.

The site is very secure. You will be prompted to provide them with security questions so that unauthorized persons won't be allowed to access your account. "What is your father's middle name?" or "What color was your first car?" are typical questions. I know some who have failed to answer the security questions correctly, or have entered the wrong password three times and were locked out of the account for a day or so. If you get totally frustrated with it, you may request that a paper statement be mailed to you or you may go to your local Social Security office, present a driver's license or some other government-issued identification, and set up your account the old-fashioned way. Once you have the account set up, you will be able to access the online version of the statement. For your protection, the password you enter must have capital letters, numbers and a keyboard symbol, such as the pound sign or ampersand. This is a pain, but I suppose it is for our protection. Either make your password something impossible for you to forget or write it down and hide it somewhere you will remember to look for it (easier said than done if you're like me), because resetting your password is a pain.

Once you are in, you can print and save the documents you see. I encourage my clients to print these before their annual review. Some tell me they were wondering why they hadn't received any statements in the mail lately. Another advantage of having an online account is that you and your advisor can access your information on the computer at the office.

What Information Will You Find?

Just like on the old paper statements, you can expect to find the following:

- Your estimated Social Security benefits available at 62, currently, at full retirement age, and at age 70
- Your annual earnings record
- How much you have paid in Social Security and Medicare taxes during your career

There is also very useful information for those who are curious as to how their benefits are calculated. I found the information to be in plain words and easy to comprehend.

How Your Social Security Benefits Are Calculated

Social Security benefits are based on the earnings on which you pay Social Security payroll taxes. The higher your earnings, up to a maximum taxable amount ($117,000 in 2014), the higher your benefits. But it is not on a dollar-for-dollar scale. As the graph here shows, workers who earned less get paid more, proportionally. Higher income earners subsidize the system for lower income earners. It's the American Way. For example, benefits for someone who earned about 45 percent of the average wage and then retired at age 65 in 2012 replace about 55 percent of his or her prior earnings. But benefits for a person who always earned the maximum taxable amount replace only 27 percent of his or her prior earnings, though they are larger in dollar terms than those for the lower-wage worker. Once someone starts receiving their Social Security benefits, they automatically are pegged to increase each year to keep pace with inflation. Most private pensions and annuities are not designed to do that.

As to how your Social Security retirement benefit is calculated, if you establish your online account, you will find the following under the "How you qualify for benefits" tab:

"To qualify for benefits, you earn 'credits' through your work — up to four each year. This year, for example, you earn one credit for each $1,200 of wages or self-employment income. When you've earned $4,800, you've earned your four credits for the year. Most people need 40 credits, earned over their working lifetime, to receive retirement benefits. For disability and survivors benefits, young people need fewer credits to be eligible.

We checked your records to see whether you have earned enough credits to qualify for benefits. If you haven't earned enough yet to qualify for any type of benefit, we can't give you a benefit estimate now. If you continue to work, we'll give you an estimate when you do qualify."

When I clicked on "How we estimated your benefits," I found this interesting information:

"If you have enough work credits, we estimated your benefit amounts using your average earnings over your working lifetime. For 2014 and later (up to retirement age), we assumed you'll continue to work and make about the same as you did in 2012 or 2013. We also included credits we assumed you earned last year and this year.

Generally, the older you are and the closer you are to retirement, the more accurate the retirement estimates will be because they are based on a longer work history with fewer uncertainties such as earnings fluctuations and future law changes. We encourage you to use our online Retirement Estimator to obtain immediate and personalized benefit estimates.

*We can't provide your actual benefit amount until you apply for benefits. And that amount **may differ** from the estimates shown below because:*

Your earnings may increase or decrease in the future.

Your actual benefits will be adjusted for cost-of-living increases.

Your estimated benefits are based on current law. The law governing benefit amounts may change. Congress has made changes to the law in the past and can do so at any time.

Your benefit amount may be affected by military service, railroad employment or pensions earned through work on which you did not pay Social Security tax."

I wish all information that came from the federal government was that easy to understand! I have to say I was favorably impressed. For those who are already receiving Social Security benefits or who are enrolled in Medicare, the online account allows them to check benefit and payment information, change their address, start or change their direct deposit information or request a benefit verification letter that can be used as proof of income when applying for a loan or for state or local benefits.

How Annual Benefits Compare to Earnings for Workers Retiring at Age 65 in 2012

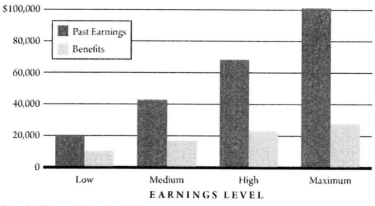

Source: Social Security Administration, 2012 Trustees Report

Center on Budget and Policy Priorities | cbpp.org

For most middle-income couples, Social Security in fact makes up from 20 to 50 percent of their retirement income and provides upwards of $500,000 in lifetime benefits. Obviously, that is a large sum of money for just about anyone. It just makes sense to maximize that asset — get the most out of it — if you can. You know, we don't hear enough about how unique Social Security is as a retirement asset. For most married couples, Social Security is the only retirement asset that:

- Is adjusted annually for inflation
- Is tax-advantaged — at worst, it's only 85 percent taxable as normal income
- Will continue to pay as long as you live
- Is backed by a government promise

With so much at stake, **when** and **how** to elect Social Security may be the most important decision middle-income couples make in retirement.

Taking Social Security Early or Late?

Most people are eligible to elect Social Security at any time between age 62 and 70. However, most people simply elect Social Security at whatever age they decide to retire, not the age when it will give them the maximum lifetime benefit.

How much you receive from Social Security depends on three primary factors:

1. Your earnings record
2. When you elect to begin benefits
3. How long you expect to live

Since you can't go back and change your earnings record, and you have minimal control over how long you live, calculating an expected lifetime benefit largely hinges on when you elect to take benefits.

In theory, if you elect early, you will get a smaller benefit for a longer period. If you elect later, you will get a larger benefit for a shorter period. For single people, the decision of whether to elect early or later is usually as simple as answering the question: do you think you'll live long enough to make waiting worth it? For example, if you decide to elect at 66, how long will it take for the larger payments to make up for the payments you missed from 62 to 65.

Single people can use a simple "break-even" calculator to determine how long they would have to live to make waiting worthwhile.

For married couples, however, the decision is much more complex.

Why? Because Social Security offers three distinct benefits for married people that these simple calculators ignore:

1. **Retired Worker Benefit:** Based on your own earnings record
2. **Spousal Benefit:** Provides your spouse with a benefit once you claim your own benefit
3. **Survivor Benefit:** Provides your spouse with a benefit after your death

Virtually all of the simple break-even calculators in use today ignore spousal and survivor benefits. More complex planning software includes spousal and survivor benefits but only for one combination of election ages. In short, neither tool offers a thorough analysis. ***Stay tuned!*** We've got a lot to say about that a few chapters later.

CHAPTER SEVEN

Is Social Security in Danger of Collapsing?

"America is the only country where a significant proportion of the population believes that professional wrestling is real but the moon landing was faked."

~ David Letterman

There are many who think the Social Security program is doomed and doesn't have a leg (pardon the pun) to stand on. They come to that conclusion for many reasons, primary among them the country's burgeoning debt and the unfunded liability with which the government's entitlement programs are saddled. I don't agree with them. Granted, the program needs fixing. But, once the repairs are made and the program undergoes a makeover, it will likely continue as part of the American financial landscape for many years to come.

Even the Social Security Administration does not deny that changes have to be made in the system if it is to continue. On the front page of the 2013 Social Security statements the following warning is printed for all to see:

About Social Security's Future...

"Social Security is a compact between generations. Since 1935, America has kept the promise of security for its workers and their families. Now, however, the Social Security system is facing serious financial problems, and action is needed soon to make sure the system will be sound when today's younger workers are ready for retirement.

"Without changes, in 2033 the Social Security Trust Fund will be able to pay only about 77 cents for each dollar of scheduled benefits. We need to resolve these issues soon to make sure Social Security continues to provide a foundation of protection for future generations."

You can see why some scramble to collect their benefits as soon as they become eligible. They want to get what they can before it all goes away. But before we panic and assume that Social Security won't be around for those who are retiring in the near future, take a deep breath and remember that the program is sound **as is** until 2033. That estimate is published by the Social Security trustees themselves. Changes are already on the drawing board to extend the retirement age, increase the amount contributed by workers into the system, reduce the amount of benefits or perhaps even a combination of all three of those measures, to preserve the program.

But the fact is that Social Security isn't going bankrupt, nor is bankruptcy really possible as the system is currently set up. Part of the misunderstanding stems from the fact that historically, Social Security has always collected more than it has paid out. CNNMoney reported in October 2010 that since 1983, Social Security has taken in more revenue than it has needed to pay out in benefits. That surplus revenue, it said, was borrowed by Uncle Sam and spent on other areas of the federal budget. In exchange, Uncle Sam promised to pay back the program with interest. How good is that promise? You have to remember the government can print money. What that does to the value of the currency is another matter.

The money the Social Security Administration collects builds up in a trust fund that collects interest. But the advancing tide of baby boomers retiring (10,000 per day) has changed that picture dramatically. By the SSAs estimate, by 2021 it's expected that insurance payments will begin to exceed income. Why? Baby boomers, during their working years were paying into the system at a brisk rate. When they retire, they will not only stop contributing to the system, they will start drawing income from it. Even then, the revenue Social Security collects each year would still be enough to pay out about three-quarters of scheduled benefits as far into the future as is foreseeable.

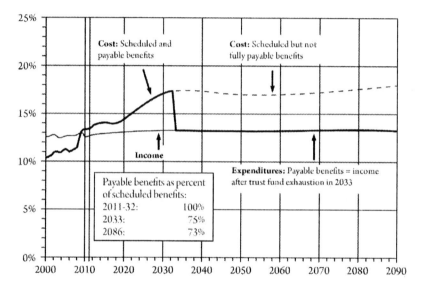

Chart source: Social Security Administration. "2012 Trustee's Report." Page 11. 2012.

So to say that Social Security is going bankrupt you would have to ignore the revenue coming into the system. Yes, there is a population bubble that is going to be putting a strain on the system for a few years, but Americans will still be going to work, collecting paychecks and paying into the system for years and years and years. Bankruptcy? Not as long as that continues. Of course, if no changes are made to the Social Security system, it wouldn't be able to meet its full obligations by 2033, but those changes will be made. Political forces that are at work even as I write this demand it. Take a deep breath, all you worriers. The Social Security system is not going bankrupt and baby boomers are grandfathered in. I have to say, however, that while boomers have nothing to worry about, people in their 30s and 40s may. That chapter hasn't been written yet.

An AARP Bulletin in June 2011 quoted the grandson of Franklin Roosevelt (the president who signed Social Security into law) on the subject of Social Security's future. He said the people who are yelling that the sky is falling today remind him of the early opponents of the SS system in the 1930s who called the program a hoax. "Purveyors of fear," he called them. Here's a quote from the younger Roosevelt that appeared in the article:

> "Social Security costs are funded out of its own dedicated revenue stream. It does not and cannot borrow money to finance its operations. There is no deficit financing... The administrative cost is .09 percent. It returns more than 99 cents to beneficiaries on every dollar collected... By the end of 2010, the Social Security trust fund had a positive balance of $2.6 trillion. As a result of interest earned on the trust fund balances, the fund's surplus will continue to expand to approximately $3.67 trillion at the end of 2022. After that year, it is projected that the balance will begin to decline. Still, reserves will be sufficient to pay full benefits through the year 2036. After that, Social Security would still be able to pay for 77 percent of benefits... This is decidedly not a program that is broke or going broke. In fact, this is quite a remarkable achievement."

I have often wondered if there is a deeper, darker political motive for the doom and gloom we hear about Social Security. Do politicians know that nothing gets the senior citizenry riled up quicker than to begin inferring that their benefits might end tomorrow? They use it as a scare tactic sometimes. "If you don't boot out the incumbent and elect me," they warn, "your Social Security benefits will be cut!"

Social Security is a sensitive topic, especially for those who are its beneficiaries, because their livelihood is on the line. One of the most talked-about faux pas ever tweeted and re-tweeted came from the Republican presidential debate held on Sept. 7, 2011, at the Ronald Reagan

Presidential Library when Texas Gov. Rick Perry called Social Security a "Ponzi scheme." He later tried to back away from the remark, but it haunted him the rest of his campaign. His rival for the nomination, Massachusetts Gov. Mitt Romney, would pounce on Perry time and again for the gaff, arguing that Perry was not only mistaken, but out of touch with older Americans.

Mitchell Zuckoff, a Boston University journalism professor who has written a book on Charles Ponzi, the man who was regarded as the King of Fraud before Bernie Madoff came along, dismisses Perry's barb outright.

"Social Security is exactly what it claims to be: A mandatory transfer payment system under which current workers are taxed on their incomes to pay benefits, with no promises of huge returns," Zuckoff said. "A Ponzi scheme is unsustainable because the number of potential investors is eventually exhausted. That's when the last people to participate are out of luck; the music stops and there's nowhere to sit. It's true that Social Security faces a huge burden — and a significant, long-term financing problem — in light of retiring baby boomers. ... But Social Security can be, and has been, tweaked and modified to reflect changes in the size of the taxpaying workforce and the number of beneficiaries."

CHAPTER EIGHT

How to Maximize Your Social Security

"Today more people believe in UFOs than believe that Social Security will take care of their retirement."

~ Scott Cook

As I have stated, some decisions you make are inconsequential. If you spend more than one minute in the morning deciding whether you need rain gear or not, you are wasting time. It will either (a) rain or (b) not. If you go prepared for rain and rain doesn't happen, it only cost you the inconvenience of carrying your umbrella and remembering to retrieve it. If you go unprepared and it happens to rain, you will do what they teach Marines to do — improvise and adapt. I doubt you will melt.

Other decisions you make, however, will be quite consequential and will affect the quality of your life for years to come if you make them incorrectly. One of those is when and how to apply for your Social Security benefits. Notice I said **when** and **how** to apply for your Social Security benefits. When to apply for your benefits is a big decision and will get a lot of attention in this book. But there are literally hundreds of possible combinations of **ways** to apply for Social Security benefits. Call them strategies. Knowing about them and executing them in a timely and effective manner can mean thousands of dollars to the average retiring couple.

The-Earlier-the-Better Myth

"The early bird gets the worm," and "the earlier the better" are two axioms that may apply to some things, but not necessarily to claiming Social Security benefits early. There is a mistaken notion that it is somehow wise to start the checks rolling in as soon as someone blows out the 62nd candle on their birthday cake. My informal poll reveals that about half of all seniors start collecting their benefits as soon as they turn 62. An article by John Wasik in the New York Times on May 14, 2014, has 41 percent of all males and 46 percent of all females applying for Social Security at age 62. Why is that? Is it a case of that other axiomatic warning: "a bird in the hand is worth two in a bush?" We have already established that Social Security isn't going to evaporate — at least not in our lifetime anyway. It could be the lingering hysteria created by the doomsayers but I don't think so. I think it has a lot to do with the word "eligible." If you are told that you are "eligible" for something, you just want to go get it, don't you? I mean, after all, you are "eligible" for it! It is yours, there for the taking! Better grab it before you *lose* your *eligibility.* I get calls all the time telling me that I am eligible for a free vacation. Even though my mind knows there is no such thing, that word, "eligible" draws me in. Few seniors I talk to who applied for their benefits early gave it much thought. The question comes up often in financial planning sessions. A typical conversation goes like this:

"I see here you list Social Security as part of your income. When did you begin taking it?"

"As soon as I became eligible — age 62."

"Why did you do that?"

"I don't know."

There is also the "monkey-see-monkey-do" syndrome. No offense is meant here. We are all guilty of this one. A golfing buddy or a close friend tells you that he or she signed up for Social Security benefits. You are both the same age. You feel as if you are missing out so, whether you need the money or not, you start asking questions about how to sign up for yours.

First, let me say there are some reasons why you may want to take your benefits as early as possible. If you are terminally ill, for example. Or if you desperately need the money to make ends meet. That is the case with some who could never save for their retirement, and I understand that. If you need the money, you need the money. But if your goal is to maximize your Social Security, you are in good health and you have other resources to fall back on, signing up early makes no sense. The way Social Security works, it will permanently lock in the lowest possible payment for life.

In the New York Times article entitled *"Social Security at 62? Let's Run the Numbers,"* Wasik makes the point that if you apply when you are 62 "you will be passing up a progressively higher benefit available in each of the next eight years. This period includes when you reach what Social Security calls your 'full retirement age' — 66 for those born between 1943 and 1954, as old as 67 for later arrivals — and what might be called a bonus period after that, ending at age 70."

Why does Wasik call the period between full retirement age and age 70 a *"**bonus** period?"* Because your benefits increase by 8 percent for every year you wait up to age 70. That's like getting a bonus! Stop and think about it. That is an extraordinary risk-free return! As I write this, interest rates are at an all-time low for guaranteed money. CDs are returning less than 1 percent. The interest rate on traditional fixed annuities are typically twice to three times that of bank CDs and their rates are low compared to what they were in years past. Unless you are getting an 8 percent compounded rate of return on a guaranteed investment somewhere, why would you not wish to use the "wait-to-take" strategy and let that 8 percent continue to accrue as long as possible? There is no sense waiting after you reach the age of 70, however. Benefits max out at that point.

The New York Times article quotes Professor Richard H. Thaler, a University of Chicago behavioral economist and Sunday New York

Times columnist: "They [early filers] are passing up a chance to increase the most cost-effective way to get more inflation-protected annuity income, which is to delay claiming. For those who are strapped for cash, it may be better to start drawing down their 401(k) assets sooner and keep building up their Social Security credits."

Who says you have to stop working at 65? Many seniors are working past their 65th birthday, not necessarily because they have to, but because they love what they do and see no reason to "hang up their spurs" just yet. If they are also contributing to a 401(k) or an IRA, this can significantly impact their retirement income picture. If you work past 62 and then collect Social Security at 70 you not only get the lifetime boost in your Social Security benefits but your IRA or 401(k) could grow significantly in those eight years. Imagine this scenario:

You are 62 and you decide to keep working until age 70 (and your employer lets you).

You earn $80,000 per year and get a 3 percent raise each year.

You have $250,000 sitting in your 401(k) (or other tax-deferred savings plan).

You continue to contribute 10 percent to it.

Your employer matches 50 percent up to 6 percent of your income.

You get a 5 percent rate of return.

By age 70, your quarter million in your 401(k) is almost a half-million ($482,000 to be exact)!

What you do is up to you, of course, and every situation is different. However, when you are dealing with money, it pays to stand back and eye your options carefully — especially if you are not sure you will have enough when you retire.

What Are Spousal Benefits?

When you have a spouse, Social Security gets more complicated. When making decisions, there are spousal benefits to consider. The way Social Security works, if you are a spouse and you have never worked a day in your life — at least not at a regular paycheck job — you will probably still be able to collect Social Security benefits. The rules state that you must be at least 62 and your spouse (or ex-spouse) must be receiving *or is eligible for* retirement or disability benefits. These are called ***spousal benefits.*** Many do not realize it, but every time you pay a dollar into the Social Security system, you are not just paying in for yourself. A portion of that contribution goes for spousal benefits whether you ever have a spouse or not.

The rules on how spousal benefits are paid are a little tricky. Let me retract that. They are *a lot* tricky! And tricky isn't really the word. That implies motive. Spousal benefit strategies are complex. What would you expect from anything orchestrated by our dear old Uncle Sam? There are literally 1,379 different strategies to choose from when electing how and when to take Social Security when spousal benefits are involved, and judging from the situations I have worked with, they are like fingerprints — no two situations are exactly alike.

> IMPORTANT NOTE: The people at the Social Security Administration have little or no training in strategies. Don't bother asking them to explain strategies to you. You will either get no advice or the wrong advice. This is no reflection on these hard-working public servants. I'm sure they are fine people. It is just not their job to sift through all the thousands of permutations and possible scenarios and come up with solutions for you. Most financial advisors are not capable of advising you on optimizing your Social Security benefits either. It is a little like the medical profession. You have to specialize in it to understand it. You must deal with it every day before you can competently diagnose the situation and prescribe a strategy. It is probably worthwhile to talk to a competent financial advisor who is fully trained and current on Social Security to see how to reap the maximum benefits if a spouse is involved.

We live in the age of computers and sophisticated software programs. These programs are able to take raw data obtained from the Social Security statement, combined with other income data and objectives and quickly sort through all the permutations of benefit claiming options available and spit out a recommendation. The analysis we can perform now is capable of quantifying exactly how much one strategy will yield in comparison with another. The result, of course, is an improved financial situation and an enhanced income picture in retirement. For some couples, just knowing what to do and when to do it has made hundreds of thousands of dollars of difference. I have seen cases where a spouse who produced the most income and had already started Social Security benefits could suspend those benefits upon reaching full retirement age (usually age 66), and then restart them when they reached age 70 and in so doing add tens of thousands of dollars to their bottom line.

Switching Strategies

What many seniors do not realize is that if you file for your Social Security benefits prior to your full retirement age you are deemed to have filed for *all benefits for which you are eligible.* At full retirement age and beyond, however, you have several options to elect a limited benefit for a period, and then convert to larger benefit at some point in the future. Would it surprise you to learn that these options represent more than $10 billion in unclaimed Social Security benefits? It is not uncommon for an individual family putting certain strategies to work to receive an additional $20,000 to $40,000 in benefits.

The approach of switching strategies takes advantage of two basic techniques: "the restricted application" and the "file and suspend" technique. When you go to your local Social Security office for help in maximizing your benefits, you may meet with some very nice people who have been trained to help you identify the highest benefit you can get *today* — not necessarily over your *lifetime.* From my experience, they definitely aren't trained to identify strategies to help you get the highest benefits over the joint lives of both you and your spouse. Most people are not acquainted with these techniques. Don't be surprised if you encounter a puzzled look and a wrinkled brow when you ask about them.

Restricted Applications

Once you reach normal retirement age, you have the option to restrict your application to exclude certain benefits. Why on earth would you want to do that? Simple. If a benefit is excluded, it will continue to build those delayed retirement credits we have been talking about. For example, a higher-earning spouse who may want to wait until age 70 to collect his own benefit may be able to file at 66 for only the benefit available under his or her spouse's work record, while still allowing his or her own benefit to build delayed retirement credits. At age 70, he or she would switch to his own benefit. Alternatively, a lower earning spouse could restrict his or her application to only spousal benefits while continuing to claim delayed credits on his or her own earnings record.

The "File and Suspend" Strategy

One strategy that married couples have found valuable is "file and suspend." This option allows a couple to take advantage of spousal benefits while allowing the delayed retirement credits to accumulate at the same time.

The way the rules work, a spouse cannot claim a spousal benefit unless the main beneficiary claims benefits first. But wait a minute! If the main beneficiary (usually the highest income earner) claims first and begins receiving benefits, he or she misses the "bonus" of benefits increasing 8 percent per year until age 70! That is where the "suspend" part comes in. Once full retirement age is reached (age 66 for those born between 1943 and 1954), a main beneficiary can file for benefits but then immediately suspend receipt of those benefits until some future date. By doing this, his or her spouse can claim a spousal benefit and the main beneficiary can let his or her own retirement benefit grow at 8 percent per year. Also, if both spouses have reached full retirement age, it is possible for the spouse's own benefit to grow (due to delayed requirement credits) if he or she decides to receive free spousal benefits. This is also called the "restricted application option."

What many married (and even divorced) people do not understand is that when applying for Social Security benefits they have a choice to make. Upon reaching full retirement age, they are eligible for both a *retirement* benefit and a *spousal* (dependent) benefit. Their first option is to claim either (a) their regular Social Security benefit or (b) their Social Security spousal benefit — with the ability to switch to their regular retirement benefit later on. *Option B* is known as a restricted application for spousal benefits. You apply for Social Security but you *restrict* your claim to your spousal benefits only.

Here's an example: Let say that Bob and Ann just reached their full retirement age, which in this case is age 66. Bob wants to continue working until he is 70. Ann wants to retire. Bob's Social Security check would be $2,000 per month if he claimed at age 66. Ann's Social Security retirement benefits are $900. If Ann could claim *spousal benefits,* however, her monthly check would be $1,000. Why? That is exactly half of her husband's age-66 benefit. But Ann can't claim a spousal benefit unless Bob files for his own retirement benefits. At first, Bob didn't want to file for his benefits at age 66 because he wanted to let his benefit amount grow until he reached 70. He saw on his Social Security statement that, if he waited until then, his benefits would be $2,640 per month — his delayed retirement credits in action!

Then Bob discovered that he could file for his benefits at age 66 and then immediately *suspend* them, in other words not actually receive them, and this would open the way for Ann to receive half of the benefits he would have received, had he taken them. Problem solved. His benefits will continue to accrue credits. He will still get his full $2,640 per month at age 70. Ann gets her $1,000 per month. Since she is taking not her own benefits but spousal benefits under Bob, her own benefits get delayed retirement credits until she reaches 70. At age 70, her monthly retirement benefits based on her own earnings record will be $1,188 (=$900×1.32).

Couples Separated by Age

What about couples where one person has reached full retirement age and the other hasn't? Will the "file and suspend strategy" work for them? It can with certain caveats. The benefit of the main beneficiary will continue to grow, but the spouse's benefit will not. The advantage to the spouse, however, is that he or she has the opportunity to draw a spousal benefit in addition to his or her own benefit when the file and suspend strategy is used. Here's an example:

John has just reached his full retirement age of 66. His wife, Susan, will turn 62 in a couple of months. John's monthly Social Security benefit is $2000 a month. Susan had a limited earnings history. When she turns 66, her full retirement benefit would be $400 per month. But Susan wants to retire and start receiving benefits at age 62 while John continues to work until he reaches age 70. If Susan just claims her own retirement benefits at age 62, she will only receive $300 per month because of the early retirement penalty ($400 x 0.75). John, however, can "file and suspend," that is, file for his own retirement benefits and then suspend receipt of them until age 70. He earns delayed retirement credits until his age 70 and Susan can now claim spousal benefits of $720 per month at her age 62.

Susan's own benefits, small though they may be in comparison to John's, will be $300 per month PLUS a 70 percent of the spousal benefit available to her, or $420. Meanwhile, John's benefits grow to at least $2,640 because of his delayed retirement credits.

Is the file and suspend strategy always the smartest move for married couples? Not always. There are many factors you need to take into consideration. The only accurate answer is "it depends." While Social Security rules are the same for everyone, no two people, or two couples, have the same retirement goals and income needs. Why not feed your information into the computer and let the machine do its magic? One thing is abundantly clear, however: Social Security, according to the way the rules are spelled out, rewards those who wait and those who know and understand their options.

Divorced Individuals

Most of the literature on retirement that crosses my desk at Sandy Morris Financial Services has photographs of happy, gray-haired couples walking hand-in-hand on the beach, strolling through a sun-splashed garden, smiling, picking flowers or playing Frisbee with grandkids. You think, "I'll bet these people never say a cross word to each other." The truth is, more than 50 percent of all marriages these days end in divorce. Happy thoughts or not, it's the way things are. So what about divorced people? What Social Security provisions exist for them?

In most cases, divorced spouses can still make claims for Social Security benefits using their ex-spouse's work history. There are some caveats. Your ex-spouse must still be alive. You have to have been married to your ex-spouse for at least 10 years, and you must not have remarried. It does not matter if your ex-spouse has remarried. Your ex-spouse must have filed for benefits, or, if not, you must have been divorced for at least two years. Your ex-spouse must be eligible for Social Security (be at least age 62).

Let's use this example: A woman who was formerly married wants to retire at age 66. She and her ex-husband are eligible for a $2,000 per month retirement benefit at their full retirement age. She can choose to defer her own retirement benefit and, instead, claim a spousal of 50 percent of her ex-husband's full retirement benefit based on her ex-husband as long as she has reached her full retirement age.

You can also be eligible for survivors' benefits based on your ex-spouse's work history after your ex-spouse dies, and you can even keep receiving them if you remarry as long as you wait until age 60 or older before remarrying.

It is a little complicated, I know. The woman used in the example above will need to make some decisions. Will receiving half of her ex-husband's benefit see her through, or will she not be able to make ends meet? If she can manage with 50 percent of her ex-husband's benefits, she can then file a restricted application and let her own Social Security benefit continue to grow until she reaches age 70. If her own benefit was, say, $2,000 at age 66, and she used the "file and suspend" strategy with a restricted application, her benefit would grow to $2,640 by the time she switched from her ex-husband's benefits to her own at age 70.[1]

More Money Now

One mistake I see people make when they are evaluating the option to suspend Social Security benefits is they assume it only increases their income down the road. If you do it right, good Social Security planning often helps you find more money to spend right now. One key piece of information you must come up with is how much money you feel you will need as you go through your retirement. Once you have that figure in mind, the objective is to see how much of those living expenses can be cared for with your Social Security while we leave your other savings working for you. The less of your own savings and investments you can touch while keeping your standard of living the same, the more financially secure your overall retirement will be.

---

[1] Pacific Life. August 2013. "Social Security Strategies: The Restricted Application for Spousal Benefits."

CHAPTER NINE

Making Smart Decisions – What's at Stake?

"The system is not intended as a substitute for private savings, pension plans and insurance protection. It is, rather, intended as the foundation upon which these other forms of protection can be soundly built."

~ President Dwight D. Eisenhower on Social Security, Jan. 14, 1954

A client couple once told me about their do-it-yourself experience involving a puppy a friend had given them. The puppy — a cute-as-a-button chow/Labrador retriever mix — did indeed come without cost, but a backyard fence cost them $2,500 and an incident with a doggie door cost them about as much. After stroking a check for the fence, the man decided he would install the pet door himself. He went down to the Mega Big Hardware store, purchased all the necessary items and went to work. The instructions made the job look easy. Remove door. Cut rectangular hole in bottom of door. Install pet door. Re-hang door. Everything went fine until he went to re-hang the door and discovered the pet door was on the top, not the bottom, of the door. Undaunted, he bought another door and went at it again. He ruined the second door by cutting the hole too big. After the second try, they waved the white flag of surrender and hired the job done. By their conservative estimate the "free puppy," whom they named "Checkbook," by the way, has so far cost them somewhere in the neighborhood of $4,000.

Do-it-yourself Social Security planning is usually not such a good idea. Failing to understand the complexities of it all, many people decide to make their Social Security decisions without seeking professional advice. They have that right, of course. This is America — the land of the free — but the smartest decisions are nearly always made by those who obtain professional counsel first. Why is this the case? Because there are so many options, possibilities, strategies and combinations of strategies out there. The only way to effectively determine the best decision possible in your individual case is to work with a financial advisor who has access to modern computer software capable of analyzing hundreds of election age combinations and determine which strategy is best for you.

I have been at this a while now and I am constantly amazed when I run the numbers at how much difference *timing* makes when it comes to planning for Social Security. Would it surprise you to learn that, when examined over the long haul, the difference between the best and worst possible decisions can be well over $100,000? To get to the best possible decision we start with an analysis. This is where we feed data to the computer and see what our best options are.

The Analysis

I call the report we generate for clients "Your Social Security Timing Report," because it is all about timing. As with any other analysis, we start with data. The questionnaire begins with the standard personal information, a key piece of which is your date of birth. This is critically important to the process because the claiming system is built around full retirement age. Your full retirement age is 66 to 67, depending on your year of birth. Once you know your full retirement age, you can decide whether you want to receive a reduced benefit earlier (as early as age 62), a full benefit at full retirement age, or an increased benefit by waiting beyond your full retirement age.

If you were born in	Your full retirement age is
1943-1954	66
1955	66 and 2 months
1956	66 and 4 months
1957	66 and 6 months
1958	66 and 8 months
1959	66 and 10 months
1960 or later	67

Note: If you were born on Jan. 1 of any year, refer to the previous year to determine your full retirement age.

How Much Will You Get at Various Ages?

At full retirement age, you will be eligible for a full Social Security benefit, provided, of course, that you have worked in a job covered by Social Security and meet other eligibility requirements.

Earlier than full retirement age — As discussed in Chapter Six, you can file for benefits as early as age 62, but your Social Security benefit will be less than if you had waited until your full retirement age. Specifically, your benefits will be reduced by 5/9 of 1 percent for every month between your retirement date and your full retirement age, up to 36 months, then 5/12 of 1 percent thereafter.

For example, if your full retirement age is 66, then you will receive about 25 percent less than your full retirement benefit if you file for benefits at age 62. If your full retirement age is 67, you will receive 32 percent less by filing early. One thing most people don't seem to understand is **this reduction is permanent.** You won't be eligible for a benefit increase once you reach your full retirement age.

Later than full retirement age — You permanently increase your Social Security retirement benefit by a predetermined percentage for each month that you delay receiving them past your full retirement age (up to the maximum age of 70). How much? The annual percentage is 8 percent, but to break it down monthly, it comes out to 2/3 of 1 percent. For instance, if your full retirement age is 66 and you delay receiving benefits for four years, your benefit at age 70 will be 32 percent higher than at age 66.

Other Necessary Data

For the analysis to tell you what you need to know it needs more data. You are interested in the answer to two questions. When and how should I start collecting my Social Security? There is no simple answer. It depends on other factors which will be computed when we feed the answers to the following questions into the program:

- At what age will you stop working?
- What is your anticipated annual income after 62?
- Have you already elected to receive benefits?
- Do you have a pension from work apart from Social Security? If so, what is the benefit age in terms of years and months and how much will you receive?
- How much do you have in terms of net investible assets?
- What is your desired monthly income in retirement?
- Should one spouse die, what is the desired income of the surviving spouse?

Your Social Security Statement

The next item we need to perform an accurate analysis and answer the **when** and **how** questions is a copy of your annual statement from the Social Security Administration. I call this report the "green letter" because of the heavy green bar that underlines the words, "Your Social Security Statement" at the top and appears on each page of the document. Once a year the SSA produces your Social Security statement. As previously mentioned, the SSA used to mail these out to each SS beneficiary. Most people now access them through their online account.

May I suggest that you obtain this document each year and file it away in your records? This document contains all the information the analysis program needs to bring your individual Social Security benefits picture into clear focus (see Chapter Six, "Social Security — A National Treasure," subheading, "Setting up Your Social Security Account"). The first time I looked at one of these statements I was amazed at how well Uncle Sam keeps track of our earnings history down through the years. Every year is right there from your first job to the one at which you are currently working. The earnings history of the report accounts for every dollar paid into the system.

Some are not aware that wage earners do not automatically qualify for Social Security retirement benefits. The SSA goes by "quarters worked." Years are divided into fourths for easy calculation. Workers must pay a minimum level of Social Security taxes for at least 40 quarters (for those born after 1929) during their working lives. These 40 quarters do not have to be consecutive. The minimum level is an adjustable amount. In 2014, for instance, you received one credit for each $1,200 of earnings, up to the maximum of four credits per year. In 2005 the minimum was $900. Once you have worked and paid Social Security taxes for the required 40 quarters, you are deemed fully qualified to receive Social Security retirement benefits. Each year the amount of earnings needed for credits goes up slightly as average earnings levels increase. The credits you earn remain on your Social Security record even if you change jobs or have no earnings for a while.

You may want to make sure that the information on your Social Security statement is correct. Each year your employer sends a copy of your W-2 (Wage and Tax Statement) to Social Security. They compare your name and SS number with the name and number on your records and record your earnings on your lifelong earnings record. This is the information they use to figure your benefits. Do mistakes occur? Not often, but yes. I know of a case involving a couple where the wife went to apply for Social Security only to discover she didn't have enough credits. She knew that wasn't right. For a three-year period during the time she had worked, her Social Security deductions were not indicated on her pay records. She was able to correct the error because she was within the three-year time period (actually three years, three months and 15 days) following the end of the calendar year in which she earned the income. As long as your Social Security earnings are reported within this time period, you'll get credit towards future Social Security benefits. If your earnings are not reported within this time period, you will not accumulate any Social Security credits for the unreported income.

The "Timing Report"

Once we have fed the program the data it needs, we press the button, listen for the click and whirr, and *Voila!* Your individual Timing Report is generated. What does it contain?

Page One — Assumptions

This is a computation of your benefits but laid out in such a way as to address your individual situation. The reason it is labeled "Assumptions" is because the program is going to present a strategy two pages later based on the data you have fed into it. It makes this strategy suggestion (the **when** and the **how**) based on what it "assumes" to be the true and accurate snapshot of your financial situation in retirement. The term "assumptions" is used in science experimentation and debating. Assumptions are statements of fact that act as a basis for a conclusion.

Take a sample couple we will call Sam and Betty Jones. Page one has Sam as a male, born Dec. 12, 1955, which makes his full retirement age 66 years and 2 months. Page one lists his wife, Betty, as a female born Nov. 6, 1951, which puts her full retirement age at exactly 66. They tell the computer they need income of $5,833 per month, or nearly $70,000 per year. The program reads that data and works with that figure to answer the questions about **when** and **how** you should file for your Social Security benefits.

To make this easy for Sam and Betty to grasp, the program produces a timeline, showing Sam and Betty how much their income will be at each age from the year they are eligible (62) until age 70 when they have reached their full potential for delayed retirement credits. Here's the way it looks for Sam and Betty Jones:

Age	62	63	64	65	66	67	68	69	70
Sam	$1,768	$1,940	$2,156	$2,389	$2,633	$2,920	$3,227	$3,548	$3,886
Betty	$1,374	$1,480	$1,648	$1,824	$2,009	$2,231	$2,463	$2,707	$2,962

When laid side by side, the estimated benefits on the Timing Report will differ a bit from the income projections on the Social Security Statement. The analysis takes into consideration such factors as inflation (projected at 2.80 percent) and adjusts the formulas in the benefit calculation. The program also assumes that the average wage will increase at the same pace as inflation and adjusts your earnings during your remaining working years and the formulas for future election years accordingly.

Your Social Security Statement does not include cost-of-living adjustments. Historically, the cost of living changes regularly and the program assumes this will continue. A 2013 Social Security Trustees report (http://www.ssa.gov/oact/tr/2013/) assumes long-term cost-of-living adjustments to be between 1.8 and 3.8 percent per year with the most likely average being 2.8 percent per year.[2] We see no reason not to build that into the math.

Page Two — Strategy Comparisons

Here is where we give Sam and Betty a bird's eye view, or the lifetime income view of their Social Security benefits. This is where we get into what is known as the "break even" computation.

The first piece of decision-making information we give the couple on this page is their *expected lifetime family benefit.* This is presented using two points of reference: (1) What would the expected lifetime

---

[2] Social Security Administration. 2013. "The 2013 OASDI Trustees Report." http://www.ssa.gov/oact/tr/2013/. Accessed June 4, 2015.

family benefit be if the couple decided to apply for their benefits at the earliest possible time based on their eligibility, and (2) what would the expected lifetime family benefit be if the couple used the suggested strategy that appears on the following page.

The difference between the two strategies is considerable. The earliest available combination would yield them **$653,559** over their projected lifetimes. The suggested strategy would yield them **$709,118** over their projected lifetimes. Would $55,559 make a difference in the quality of their retirement? Then the choice is obvious unless compelling reasons dictate otherwise.

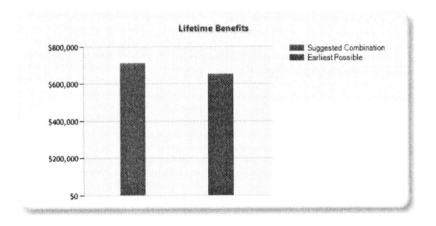

What Is Your Break-Even Age?

The next piece of important information on page two of the Timing Report is the "break-even age." Knowing this enables you to compare the long-term financial consequences of starting benefits at one age versus another. Your break-even age is the age at which the total accumulated value of your retirement benefits taken at one age equals the value of your benefits taken at a second age.

No one knows how long he or she will live; but we have to estimate it to make a smart decision. To do this, we use the research that is available to us and make as solid a projection as possible. According to a 2013 report, a man who reaches age 65 today can expect to live, on average, until approximately age 83.[3] A woman who reaches age 65 can expect to live, on average, until approximately age 85. Of course, many factors can affect this number, but in general you will reach your break-even age about 12 years from your full retirement age if taxes and inflation aren't accounted for. For example, if you start receiving benefits at age 62, and your full retirement age is 66, you will generally reach your break-even age at 78 — give or take. However, unless you're able to invest your benefits rather than use them for living expenses, your break-even age is probably not the most important part of the equation. For many people, what really counts is how much they'll receive each month, rather than how much they'll accumulate over many years.

Planning for Your Maximum Life Span

May I make a suggestion? Unless you have information to the contrary, why not plan for your maximum lifespan? That way you reduce the risk that you run out of money in your old age. The Social Security Administration estimates that one out of every four retirees will live past age 90. One in 10 will live past age 95. If you can stand to wait a few years before taking your benefits so that you will receive a higher monthly benefit for life, why not do so? Don't forget, along with that comes annual cost-of-living adjustments if prices rise. Not many other sources of income are guaranteed to keep up with inflation. Will that be there for our children and grandchildren? Perhaps not. From all I can see, however, looks like baby boomers are "grandfathered" in.

The "Break Even Chart" for Sam and Betty illustrates which of the outlined strategies that appear on page three of the report provides the best outcome at any given set of whole year death age combinations. Break-even points occur at combinations where the strategy offering the best outcome changes. The suggested strategy was determined by assuming Sam dies at 80 years 5 months and Betty dies at 84 years 3 months.

---

[3] Center for Disease Control. "2013 National Vital Statistics Report." Volume 61. Number 4. May 2013.

Break Even Chart

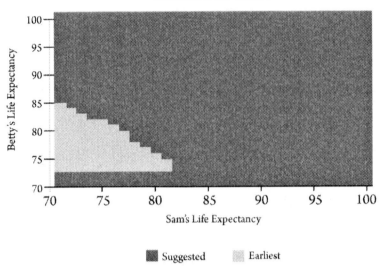

Sam's Life Expectancy

■ Suggested   ▨ Earliest

Page Three — Your Suggested Social Security Strategy

This is where, as they say, the "rubber meets the road." Here is where we answer the **when** and **how** question. Based on the data they supplied, the computer uses the assumptions to recommend the following:

- **SAM** — File a restricted application for only your spousal benefit based on Betty's earnings record at your age 66 years 2 months. This allows you to continue to earn delayed retirement credits on your own benefit. Your approximate spousal benefit would be $1,153. File for your own benefit at age 69 years. Your approximate benefit on your own earnings record would be $3,548.

- **BETTY** — File a standard application for benefits at age 68 years. Your approximate monthly benefit would be $2,463. The expected lifetime family benefit using this strategy is: $709,118.

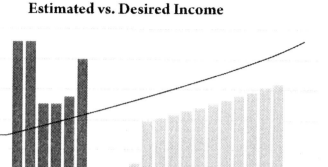

Estimated vs. Desired Income

Desired Income ■ Earned Income ▦ Social Security Income

This chart demonstrates future value cash flows using the suggested election ages and the assumptions provided. While it doesn't include taxes or other sources of income, it gives a clear picture of how the desired income can be measured, one option versus another.

Pages Four and Five — Individualized Spreadsheet

This portion of the Timing Report provides an individualized spreadsheet showing the breakdown of Social Security benefits projected for Sam and Betty. One chart shows the estimated cash flow for the suggested strategy and the other shows the estimated cash flow for the earliest possible strategy. The spreadsheets are organized by year, showing the income each individual stands to receive as the years go by. The spreadsheets are also organized by category, showing whether the Social Security income is retirement benefits or spousal benefits. To the far right of the report is another very useful section headed "Summary." This column shows the income totals and also contains a column, headed "Gap," to inform the retiring couple how far their retirement benefits will carry them and how much they will need from other sources.

Readers may have a question at this point. Why show a spreadsheet with elaborate calculations on the **earliest possible** strategy? Haven't we already established that, unless there are life-expectancy reasons involved, it is best to wait and let the benefits grow? Not always, as the following chapter will explain.

CHAPTER TEN

Other Options Involving Social Security

"The question isn't at what age I want to retire, it's at what income."

~ George Foreman

The type of financial planning I do is like a box of chocolates — you never know what you're going to get... that is, you never know what kind of solution presents itself after all that comes up in the way of solutions (my apologies to "Forrest Gump"). There are so many combinations, avenues of approach and strategies. There is no cookie-cutter solution; no one size fits all. Each case is as individual as a fingerprint.

In chapters previous to this one I have preached about maximizing your Social Security and pointed out ways to do it, especially with couples using the file-and-suspend strategy with restricted applications. Those are all valid approaches and they may fit your situation to a tee, but there are other strategies that I would be remiss if I didn't mention as prospects that at least deserve your consideration. One involves a 180-degree turn from waiting until the fruit on your Social Security reaches its full ripeness. Just the opposite, in fact, is called for in this possible approach.

Max-Funded Indexed Universal Life Insurance

Two of the most powerful words in the English language are "what" and "if." When you put them together you can see so many possibilities, especially in planning for life after 50.

What if, instead of maximizing your Social Security by waiting until age 70 to take it, you filed for it at age 62 and used the money to maximum fund an indexed universal life policy? Sure, you would only receive 75 percent of your full retirement age benefit. However, would that really matter if you were able to take that early Social Security income and parlay it into a bigger payout down the road — perhaps even amounting to more money than you would have received by waiting until 70 to collect your Social Security?

As Ricky Ricardo said to Lucy, "You've got some 'splaining to do!" What exactly is indexed universal life insurance and how would such a strategy work?

First of all, let me emphasize that I am not recommending this strategy for everyone. Some may not be comfortable with it and others may not qualify for it. But it is one more tool in our financial toolbox and we need to know how it works. Secondly, when you say the word insurance, people have a tendency to get up and leave the room. Stay with me here. It's not what you think. To properly explain I have to start at the beginning.

The Birth of Life Insurance

Life insurance has been around since the days of the ancient Romans. Soldiers got together and pooled their money so that, in case they died in battle, they could get a decent burial. They called them "burial clubs." Roman soldiers believed the gods would not allow them into the afterlife without a proper burial, and funerals cost money. That basic idea grew into a fund to care for the families of slain soldiers, incorporating one of the basic tenets of life insurance — sharing of risk.

I am not sure what happened to life insurance during the Dark Ages. If it survived as a concept, I imagine the bubonic plague wiped it out as an enterprise.

The idea of life insurance was resurrected in London, England, when Edmond Halley developed the first life expectancy table. He also figured out a way to compute the orbit of the comet that bears his name — but that's another story. Now that Halley could predict human mortality, he could combine those statistics with the principles of compound interest and make a profit selling simple life insurance policies and the insurance industry was born.

America has the Presbyterian Church to thank for its life insurance industry. In 1759, the Presbyterian Synod of Philadelphia was the first to sponsor a life insurance program for ministers and their families. Believe it or not, many other religious groups in America frowned on the idea because it seemed to them like gambling. "Betting against God," they called it. By the middle of the 1800s, that notion faded and life insurance became more acceptable to Americans. Insurance companies marketed it by appealing to the "moral duty" of husbands to provide for their families if they were to die prematurely.[4]

The Two Kinds of Life Insurance

We buy homeowners insurance to replace our home if it burns down. We buy life insurance to replace the money our life is worth to our loved ones. When you put it that way, it sounds ridiculous, doesn't it? You cannot put a price on a life, can you? Well, from a business standpoint, you actually can. The original idea was to replace your earnings capability if your life ended prematurely. You pay a monthly premium (small amount) and if you die the insurance company pays a death benefit (big amount). It's all about spreading the risk. Essentially, there are two kinds of life insurance: term and whole life.

---

[4] Brian Anderson. LifeHealthPro. Sept. 1, 2011. "The Origins of an Industry." http://www.lifehealthpro.com/2011/09/01/the-origins-of-an-industry. Accessed June 4, 2015.

Term means what it says. You pay premiums for 10, 15, 20 years — ostensibly during the peak earning years of your life — in return for the promise of the insurance company to send your family a death benefit check should you die *within that term*. Once that term expires and you are still around, your policy ends. Thanks for playing, but if you want to keep the coverage, you must buy a new policy based on your current age — more costly now because you are older. There are all kinds of variations on this theme, but that is the essence of it.

Whole life is the opposite of term. The policy is good for the whole of your life and therefore it is costlier. You either pay more in higher premiums or have lower benefits. The insurance company is aware of the fact that you will eventually die. At some point, someone got the bright marketing idea to allow part of the life insurance premium to go for building cash value from investments made by the insurance company. Kind of like a forced savings program. The cash value would build tax-deferred each year and, because of tax rules, you could borrow against the cash accumulation fund without being taxed.

Along Comes Universal Life

In the early 1980s, when interest rates were at an all-time high, people began dumping their whole life policies left and right. It didn't help matters that the Federal Trade Commission issued a report criticizing whole life for its below-market returns. The prime rate was at 11.75 percent to start the year, and ended at 15.25 percent (and peaked at 21.5 percent in December 1980). Meanwhile the interest rates on whole life policies were stuck in low single digits. There was a movement underway in those days known as "buy term and invest the difference." The idea was that it made sense to cash in your whole life policies, with their paltry rates of return, and invest the money in either the stock market or bank CDs. Buy a term policy to replace the insurance part and you are leagues ahead.

Make no mistake about one thing: insurance companies are driven by profit. That's why they have so many buildings with their names at

the top of them. To regain their competitive edge, in 1979 they introduced a new kind of insurance known as universal life. It combined
permanent insurance with a different type of cash growth feature. Instead of a return arbitrarily set by the insurance company, this cash value
component's return would float with the value of Treasury bills. The
premium would be flexible, too. As long as the policy expenses were
met, you could overpay some months and skip others. You could even
buy a universal life policy with a single lump sum premium if you wanted to.

To attract investors, insurance companies touted the advantages of
tax-deferred saving and tax-free loans. The way the IRS looked at the
cash value inside a universal life policy, it was a reserve to pay future
claims. This handy little tax provision meant that you could borrow
money from your policy's cash value tax-free and conveniently not pay it
back. This was the insurance industry's answer to the buy-term-and-
invest-the-difference movement. The economy is constantly changing,
however. Treasury bills would never yield as much in the decades that
followed as they did in the 1980s. At that time, they were at an all-time
high. However, as inflation cooled and interest rates leveled off, Treasury bills became less attractive as the foundation for the cash accumulation component for universal life policies. The new transparency and
flexibility of life policies had made them popular again but falling T-bill
yields meant a trip back to the drawing board.

Along Comes Indexed Universal Life

Enter a new, improved version of universal life called **indexed universal life,** or IUL for short. It was first introduced in 1997 when the stock
market knew only one direction — up. The basic idea was to keep all the
attractive attributes of universal life insurance but change the crediting
method to the cash accumulation element so that it reflected the upward
movement of the stock market but with no risk. Your earnings would be
gauged by a stock market index (thus the term) like the S&P 500 stock
market index. When the index went up, your cash value would grow

accordingly. When it went down, your cash value wouldn't grow much, but at least it wouldn't lose. They would call this the "ratchet/reset" feature. There would be a floor so that your cash value would always grow by a percent or two even if the market was on the skids. There would be a ceiling, too. If the index shot up 30 percent in one year you would "cap out" at, say, 15 percent. The floor and ceiling could change every year.

This is a broad-brush explanation of indexed universal life insurance — a view from 30,000 feet up. There are several more moving parts, but those are the essentials. Now that nail is in the plank, how could an IUL be used as part of a strategy where you would claim Social Security benefits as early as possible?

That brings us to the original question:

What if, instead of **maximizing** your Social Security, you filed for it as early as possible, took the lesser amount and overfunded an IUL, thus parlaying your SS benefits into a handsome, tax-advantaged retirement income down the road?

How would that work? Why would you want to "overfund" anything?

In this case, you are using the structure of the IUL policy and its built-in tax advantages to build wealth. To "overfund" an indexed universal life insurance policy means to maximize the policy's cash value growth potential and to minimize its net insurance costs over time. It is like stoking the boiler of the wealth-producing locomotive that, like all compounding, starts slow and gathers volume over time. When you pay the maximum premium into an IUL policy (overfund it), cash values grow faster. Remember, even though an IUL policy comes with a death benefit, that is not the reason we are buying it. We want to pump every dollar of the early Social Security benefit into the policy so that money will grow tax-deferred, compounded according to the upward movement of the stock market.

To make this strategy work, you want to choose the smallest life insurance death benefit possible to achieve the highest return possible on the premium payments you are able to make over a given period. One of the key advantages of a universal life policy is its flexibility. You want to consult a competent financial professional who is licensed, knowledgeable and fully trained in the workings of IUL insurance — one who will be able to develop an illustration that lays out specifically how the policy might play out over 10 years.

This strategy is not for everyone. Life insurance requires a physical examination and the applicant must be in good health in order to qualify. It is a good idea to make sure you understand all the details of any strategy before employing it. A financial advisor who is familiar with how investment-grade life insurance works will be able to answer all your questions about this strategy and help you determine if it is suitable for your financial situation.

CHAPTER ELEVEN

Attitudes Toward Retirement

"You are only young once, but you can stay immature indefinitely."

~ Ogden Nash

When people come to visit my office, I usually know what's on their minds. No, I'm not a mind reader, but everyone who is contemplating retirement is aware that they are stepping over into uncharted territory — at least uncharted by them. They want to be sure of their footing and they need a guide. They are seeking answers to hard questions. They need someone to show them all the facts so they can make intelligent choices.

One of the reasons I chose "Decisions Over 50" as part of the title of this book is because 50 seems to be the age when people begin thinking seriously about their retirement. I think it starts to dawn on people when they reach the half-century mark that their hourglass is no longer top-heavy with sand and that time is a precious commodity. Age 50 is usually the point when they begin to appreciate softer music and quieter settings. It's when people learn to sip and savor their lives instead of gulping them down.

There are all categories of attitudes toward financial planning for retirement:

The Procrastinators

These are the folks who get a flash from time to time about the future and give it a moment of intense thought, fully intending to start looking into whether they are on track to safely retire, but put it off until a tomorrow that never comes. The procrastinator has a momentary impulse to start ironing out an income plan for retirement, but just the thought of doing anything that includes the phrase "ironing out" causes them to break out in a cold sweat. They quickly divert their attention to something much less stressful. Procrastinators are great on meaning to and lousy on following through. They usually know this is a personality flaw and they fully intend to change. Maybe they'll buy a book on the subject... one of these days.

I attended a seminar once where the speaker handed out to everyone in attendance a wooden disc, about the size of a half-dollar, with the words "TUIT" on both sides. "Have you ever had something that you were putting off until you got around to it?" he asked the crowd. Heads nodded. "Well, you now have 'a round TUIT'," he said. "So DO IT!" In all my years of financial planning, I have never had one person say, "Sandy, we started this process way too early." But I have had plenty of them tell me, "I wish I had met you 10 years ago, Sandy," or words to that effect. If you are a procrastinator, I am giving each of you a round TUIT. You know what to do.

The Delegators

These are the ones who are just too busy, usually with their work or their career, to pay attention to their personal finances. Someone else handles all of that, don't they? That's fine if they do. But no one else — and this is a general statement — will ever take as much interest in your personal financial welfare as you. It's like your health. A doctor is a medical professional you pay to give you advice. But it is up to you to eat right and get plenty of exercise. The doc can't do it for you. Delegators prefer to let someone else handle all that mundane stuff. They much prefer to make the money and let someone else manage it. This sometimes comes at a price. I know of one individual who was very successful in business and turned all of his personal financial affairs over to a stockbroker the way people turn all the legal affairs over to an attorney. Delegators are the sort who "have a person" who takes care of each area of their lives. They expect an occasional verbal report and they mentally sort that task as "accomplished" and move on to the next thing. This person didn't realize how much risk he was taking on until he had been hearing on the news that banks were failing and the stock market was falling. By the time he decided to ask his broker how his investments were doing, almost half of his considerable portfolio was gone. For placing that kind of trust in someone else to manage your personal financial affairs, I give him plus 20 points for big-picture thinking and minus 40 points for common sense.

One day a couple came to my office for their second appointment with me, which is usually when we take what I call a "financial snapshot" to see where they are in the stream of things before we start developing any strategies to get them to where they want to be. What I found remarkable was they had opened only a few of the envelopes containing their last two years' financial statements. The couple owned and managed a booming real estate and construction business. The books at the office were well organized and audited down to the penny, but their personal finances were a mess. That's just the way they rolled. I told them that if we were going to work together, we would have to be a team and they agreed to devote a little more time, at least a monthly conversation, to where their money was invested and why.

The Worriers

These are the individuals who, regardless of how much money they have saved, think it will never be enough to retire. They are usually wonderful people, but they overthink every situation, especially those involving money. They are the kind of people who check the stove several times and still worry, an hour into a road trip, if they turned off all the burners. You know who you are. Worriers will sometimes pass up several legitimate opportunities to retire, thinking they need to work one more year just to be safe. Better safe than sorry, they reason. Then, when that year is over, they decide to put in just one more year before they call it quits.

Worriers typically want guarantees, not projections, and they must see things in black and white before they relax. I remember one 64-year-old woman who had worked in the office of an engineering firm for 20 years and thought there was no way on earth she could possibly retire the following year. She had very little savings, but she had a 401(k) worth more than $300,000, and, if she waited until she was age 70 to collect it, she could expect to receive approximately $2,500 per month in Social Security. After I helped her establish a very detailed budget, the picture became clear that, given her lifestyle requirements, she could easily retire with a guaranteed income of $50,000 per year by laddering her investments and timing her income. I honestly think the woman would have worked another five years, imagining the elusive goal of a comfortable retirement was well beyond her reach. To borrow from the popular phrase, "there's an app for that," there is a "strategy for that." That is to say, there is a strategy for most of what the worriers worry about. Worriers, more than anyone else, need to sit down with a retirement income specialist and nail down the exact amount of income they can expect to have if they retire this year, next year or the year after. The worrier needs to lay all their contingency concerns out on the table and let the professional planner find a strategy to lay those concerns to rest.

The Do-It-Yourselfers

Investing is no problem for the do-it-yourselfer — until it is, of course. The DIYer is nearly always very computer savvy. He or she has a laptop, a desktop, a smart phone and a tablet and fully half the applications on these devices have to do with money. They research stocks and study charts. They take pride in their ability to understand the same terms that professional investors use and concern themselves with the intricacies of intra-day trading to the extent that they can't enjoy a lunch without checking on how their ticker symbols are doing that day on Wall Street.

I saw a clever cartoon the other day. A man dressed in a business suit was standing downtown holding a cardboard sign which read: "Need Money to Resume Day Trading." The man's turned out pockets and sad expression indicated he must have had a recent run of bad luck at the pastime. There is nothing wrong with DIY investing if you are using discretionary funds you can afford to risk. It's a fascinating hobby for many and I get that. What I am saying is that it is unwise to use funds you and your spouse need to retire on to play the market. Picking stocks and attempting to time the market is a fool's game.

The Big Spenders

The last thing to ever cross the mind of the big spender is that the money may someday run out. The big spender is constantly in debt for luxuries he or she can't afford. First base in planning for retirement is becoming debt free, except perhaps for one's own residence, and even paying off that is desirable. To the big spender, money is a never-ending stream of cash that cannot dry up. Personal finance speaker Suze Orman and I do not see eye-to-eye on everything, but I do agree with her on this: "Don't just live within your means. Live below your means and within your needs." Chapter Three of this book touched on the saving mindset versus the spending mindset.

Saving for the future should be as fundamental a fiscal habit as counting your change. I recommend that you salt away at least 10 percent of your gross income during your working years. Once you retire, I recommend maintaining a liquid emergency fund that represents at least six months' income. That way you won't be tempted to tap your "working resources," which are vital to your retirement strategies.

The Job Junkie

This character is also known as the workaholic. Addicted to the career the way some people are addicted to substances. This individual will never retire as long as they have breath in their body to crawl to a desk and a telephone. For them, their work is their life. It could be that these types honestly feel the world would stop spinning if they were to turn in their 90-day notice and stop and smell the roses.

I know of people who had the resources in place to retire years ago, but couldn't bring themselves to do it. In one instance, it was a lawn care business a man had started from scratch and built to include a large warehouse, 15 employees and 10 service vehicles. His son-in-law and daughter worked in managerial positions with the firm and he had been talking for years about turning over the reins to them... next year. Next year never came. He couldn't envision himself taking life easy. I told him that it was perfectly all right to feel that way as long as he **knew** that he was crazy. (He knew I was joking, but I kind of meant it, too. I am a firm advocate of stopping occasionally to smell the roses, no matter how in-dispensable you are!)

The Planners

And then, God bless 'em, there are those who have a pretty clear idea of what they want their retirement to look like and see the need for stra-tegic planning to get them there. Without these people, I would be out of a job, so naturally I could hug their necks. They give me purpose in life. These are the folks who understand the difference between knowledge and applied knowledge. These are the people who took sav-ing seriously enough to accumulate a nest egg for retirement and they realize that, once they take that first step past receiving a paycheck and paying themselves, they need a blueprint that will carry them for the rest of their lives. These are the ones who, although self-sufficient in many areas of life, realize they need professional help in something as complex as retirement income planning. I confess I admire many of these indi-viduals I have come to know over the years they have been my clients, and I have come to view them as friends. I will never forget what one of them told me at the end of a satisfactory annual review:

"Do you know what the difference is between knowledge, wisdom and understanding?"

"No, what is it?" I replied

"Knowledge is a collection of facts. You know, for instance, that you are standing on a railroad track. You know the train is coming."

"Okay, got it," I said.

"Understanding is seeing the relationship of the hard steel of the locomotive to the soft tissue of your body. You understand that the impact would kill you."

"Wisdom is getting the h*** off the tracks!"

Making Retirement Happen

I once saw this sign on the wall of a waiting room at an automobile dealership service center:

There are three kinds of people in the world
- Those who **MAKE** things happen
- Those who **WATCH** things happen
- Those who **WONDER** what happened

Statistics seem to indicate that a lot of Americans fall into the latter category when it comes to retirement. The Employee Benefit Research Institute (EBRI) conducts a Retirement Confidence Survey each year. The 24th annual RCS was released March 18, 2014, and revealed that only 44 percent of those surveyed say they have even tried to calculate how much money they will need to have saved in order to comfortably retire. The EBRI survey said, "few seek financial advice and fewer take it."

"Roughly one in five workers and 25 percent of retirees report they have obtained investment advice from a professional financial advisor..."

Well *that's* not too encouraging. The survey concludes with this ominous bit if information: "The percentage of workers planning to work for pay in retirement now stands at 65 percent."

I guess so. If you haven't even calculated how much money you will need in retirement, and you haven't asked for professional help, then you will probably end up on somebody's payroll when you should be enjoying your golden years.

One of the points I like to make when I am asked to speak on the subject is that retirement is just not one of those things you want to *let happen* to you. You have to be a little pro-active or things will not turn out well. In my informal survey, I find that most people, when they turn 60, know they are eligible to begin taking their Social Security as early as age 62. They get that. And they know full retirement age is age 66. That much is clear. But past that, the picture gets a little murky for them.

One pro-active step I heartily recommend for anyone over 50 is to set up their "My Social Security" account on SSA.gov. Learn how much your checks will amount to each month if you start collecting your Social Security at the various dates listed. That's making things happen. Nailing that down is one piece of the retirement puzzle. If you need help coming up with a budget for retirement, don't pace the floor. Send up a distress flare for a professional. That's what we are here for! Consultations are free, you know. The next big piece of the puzzle is the "how much" question. How much do I need to have saved in order to comfortably retire with the income I desire?

Without knowing some of those facts, I'm sorry, but it's a little like standing at an intersection, wearing a blindfold and being asked to pick the right direction.

Saving for retirement should begin when you get your first real paycheck — you know, the kind with taxes taken out and withholding subtracted from it. Planning for retirement should start when you are somewhere in your 40s. That's when you begin to crystalize your goals, and your vision of retirement is no longer a blank canvas. By that time you also have a general idea of how much you can expect to be earning by the time you are retirement age.

By the time you reach your 50s, you will be making some permanent decisions that will play out when you finally do retire. You will have an even clearer idea of where you are and where you are heading. The shift from accumulation to preservation begins to take place during these years as you slowly adjust the risk settings on your investments to safe and then safer. Your choices regarding long-term care are at an optimum here rather than later in life. Your options are multitudinous in your 50s and dwindle rapidly when you pass the age 65 mark.

CHAPTER TWELVE

Having Enough Income for the Rest of Your Life

"We can easily forgive a child who is afraid of the dark; the real trage-dy of life is when men are afraid of the light."

~ Plato

We all have our phobias. I will make you a deal…I won't ask what yours are if you don't ask me about mine! One of the longest words I have ever seen in print is "paraskavedekatriaphobia," which means fear of Friday the 13th. I know some people who stay home from work when that day rolls around. Hotels have elevators with no 13th floor. Of course there *is* a 13th floor. Just calling the 13th floor the 14th floor doesn't change the order of the floors. I am still not sure what the com-bination of Friday and the number 13 does to make that date on the cal-endar so fear-inspiring or unlucky. I hope I am not stepping any toes here, but of all the superstitions out there, that is one of the silliest.

I have heard for several years that the greatest fear of senior citizens was the fear of outliving their resources in retirement. It wasn't until I saw a survey conducted in 2010 by the Allianz Insurance Company of North America that I ever saw statistical proof. But, sure enough, fear of running out of resources in retirement outranks snakes, spiders, the number 13 and even death on the phobic scale. People may not express this fear the same way, but the meaning is clear. It is sometimes expressed by the consequence such a development might cause. Loss of independence, for example. Becoming a burden on one's family.

Technically speaking, phobias are unwarranted fears, unreasonable fears. Fears without basis in fact. The fear of outliving one's resources in old age is not a phobia. Given the statistics on retirement preparedness in the last chapter, it is a very real eventuality for some.

In Chapter One, we talked about the phenomenon of increased longevity among baby boomers. It is both a blessing and a curse. Living longer is a good thing, as long as one's quality of life is part of the package. Based on how active retiring boomers seem to be, 60 does indeed seem to be the new 40. Outliving your resources and becoming a burden on your loved ones is probably not the storybook ending you had in mind for your retirement, but according to a survey released in July 2014 by the Federal Reserve, many Americans facing retirement are heading in that direction. If the sampling accurately reflects the nation's retirement readiness, the picture isn't a pretty one. The poll asked 3,051 households the following question: "How are you and your spouse planning to pay for expenses in retirement?" The answers included:

- Social Security/ old-age benefits — 44.6 percent
- I will continue working — 23.5 percent
- Defined benefit pension from work — 18.5 percent
- 401(k) or 403(b) type retirement plan — 39.7 percent
- Individual retirement account (IRA) — 22.1 percent
- Savings outside a retirement account — 23.4 percent[5]

I don't know how much faith to put in such polls. The Fed survey included people over 18, and they claimed their sampling was "representative of the U.S. population." It was an email survey that asked a blue million questions and it must have taken the average respondent hours

---

[5] Federal Reserve. July 2014. "Report on the economic Well-Being of U.S. Households in 2013." http://www.federalreserve.gov/econresdata/2013-report-economic-well-being-us-households-201407.pdf. Accessed June 4, 2015.

to complete. If one came to me it would go right into my laptop's recycle bin. But the one that jumped out at me was the top one. Really? Almost half of the population of America thinks that Social Security alone will pay for their expenses in retirement? Some folks are in for a rude awakening when they hit retirement (think brick wall at 60 miles per hour), don't you think?

The American Association of Retired Persons, which prefers to go by its sleeker acronym AARP these days, likes to interview people over the age of 50, so their responses may offer a better across-the-board sampling of the mood of the nation's senior population. In their December 2010 survey, they asked people turning 65 about their attitudes toward work and retirement. I thought the responses were interesting:

- I plan to work until I drop — 40 percent
- I plan to quit working as soon as I can — 49 percent
- Don't know — 9 percent
- Refused to answer — 1 percent[6]

Here's my take on "work until you drop." If you are doing that because you have to, that's pretty sad. We need to talk. If you are doing that because you **want** to — because it gives you a sense of satisfaction and fills a vacuum in your life — then more power to you. I'm probably in the same league. By my own informal survey, however, most people who work after they reach retirement age either haven't planned properly and don't know that strategies exist to enable them to quit working, or they haven't saved adequately and are forced to continue working.

Staying Independent

A major retirement goal for most baby boomers is maintaining their independence. That was reflected in all the surveys I read. AARP report-

---

[6] AARP. December 2010. "Approaching 65: A Survey of Baby Boomers Turning 65 Years Old." http://assets.aarp.org/rgcenter/general/approaching-65.pdf. Accessed June 4, 2015.)

ed 41 percent of older Americans told their pollsters they want to stay in their own home for as long as possible and avoid the nursing home or assisted living facility if at all possible. Understandable. Survey respondents said they want to hold onto their mobility as long as possible in retirement. Driving an automobile in America is a symbol synonymous with independence.

The "sandwich generation" is a term used to describe baby boomers who find themselves caring for aged parents and returning adult children at the same time. I have no statistics on this, but personal observations (I know a few of them personally) tell me that this situation changes the financial ballgame dramatically. Here they are, getting older themselves, and their nest goes from comfortably empty to full and overflowing. Their earlier retirement goals may have been more leisure-oriented, but now they are replacing plans for dream vacations and foreign travel with visions of staying home, babysitting two generations and clipping coupons.

Such attitudes and concerns are what impelled me to become a financial planner in the first place. Growing up, I saw firsthand how a lack of education in handling financial matters can wreck one's future. The financial advisory community has done a poor job of explaining to senior citizens what options are available to them — options that could eliminate their worry about having enough income in retirement.

Once, in an interview, the reporter asked me what I felt was the most important thing I could bring to the table to help retirees who were worried about their financial future. Perhaps the reporter expected me to come up with a self-serving commercial about Sandy Morris Financial. But I didn't hesitate to say, "Education." The concerns and fears of those who are retired and those approaching retirement are legitimate, but many of them can be eased by information about safe-money investing and savings alternatives. First, let's talk about what no longer works.

The 4 Percent Rule Doesn't Work Anymore

Brokerage firms and advisors who are rooted solely in the stock market have for years touting something called the "4 Percent Withdrawal Rule" as a formula to guide their clients safely through retirement. To make the math easy, let's say that you were able to retire with $1 million. The 4 Percent Rule held that you should be able to withdraw 4 percent of that amount, or $40,000, per year to live on, add slightly to that for inflation each year, rebalance your portfolio mix of stocks and bonds each year, and that should give you an income for 30 years or the end of your life, whichever came first.

The 4 Percent Rule, or the "4 Percent Drawdown Rule," was the brainchild of three professors at Trinity University in San Antonio, Texas, in the mid-1990s. Their computations and projections were based on stock market data available at the time. But in the 1990s, the stock market was on an upward roll. In those days, you could do no wrong investing in the stock market because the charts knew only direction — north. The problems with the 4 Percent Rule are manifold. First, few people have a million dollars to play with going into retirement. Second, the market is volatile and the data collected then is no longer relevant. Third, life expectancy is on the rise and what if you want to retire early? All of that makes the formula null and void as a workable formula for a worry-free retirement. Still, in the face of all the evidence, there are some financial advisors out there that are holding onto the 4 Percent Rule and advising clients that it still works. Perhaps this is not malicious. Perhaps they haven't been reading the trade journals. Perhaps this is the only approach to investing they know and don't know how to press their "reset" button. In any case, they need to update their files.

In an article entitled "Forget the 4% Withdrawal Rule," published by Money magazine in 2014, Wade Pfau, professor of retirement income at The American College, lowers the 4 percent withdrawal projection down to 2.22 percent. That means that if you can bring $1 million to the retirement table, and you want it to last you the rest of your life, you have to ratchet your annual withdrawal down to little more than

$20,000 per year — which is fine if you are comfortable living on the border of the national poverty line.

Other headlines and excerpts that spell the end for the "Four Percent Rule" read as follows:

- **4% Rule for Retirement Withdrawals Is Golden No More** — New York Times, 2013. "Many financial advisers are rejecting the 4 percent rule as out of touch with present realities."
- **How Much to Withdraw from Retirement Savings** — Forbes Magazine, 2013. "When the 4 percent rule emerged, investment portfolios were earning about 8 percent annually. Today, they're generally in the 3 to 4 percent range."
- **Retirees May Need to Rethink 4% Rule** — AARP, 2013. "…new research by Morningstar Investment Management suggests that relying on that 4 percent rule of thumb today is risky, thanks to a market in which bond yields and dividends have hovered at record lows for years."

Guarantees vs. Projections

The question you really want to know upon your retirement is: "How much will I be able to receive in the way of income each month for the rest of my life?" When you ask that question to your financial advisor, listen carefully. Listen for words like:

- Projection
- Estimated
- Approximately
- Probability

Those words are OK if we are dealing with the weather forecast, but most retirees have cut the umbilical cord of their paychecks from work. Now they are relying on their pensions (if they are lucky enough to have one), Social Security and savings to make ends meet. Today's retirees seem more interested in words like:

- Guaranteed

- Lifetime
- Positively
- Absolutely

The Rule of 100

How you have your financial affairs arranged at this junction in your life will make the difference between whether you will get a good night's sleep every night or you will find yourself pacing the floor with worry. There is a simple rule of thumb that retirement income planners have been using for decades to facilitate retirees getting the good night's sleep option. It's called the "Rule of 100." It is very simple. Just put a percent sign after your age. That represents the percentage of your assets you should have safely invested in retirement. Subtract that number from 100 and that represents the percentage of your assets with which you may incur some risk. The Rule of 100 is more of a guideline than a hard and fast rule. Situations vary and so do risk tolerances, but this formula takes your age into consideration when it comes to investing. No one knows when the next 2008-type market correction will occur. If **all** of your assets are in the stock market and you lose half of your life's savings as a result, will you have enough to pay the bills and still not run out of money? Will you have to go back to work? Will you have to forfeit your independence and end up depending on your loved ones for subsistence? Will you run out of money in a few years? Will you have to go back to work? The next chapter will offer an alternative to the "all-in" approach of having your entire portfolio at risk in the stock market. It is a strategy that is not for everyone and one that has a few moving parts. But it is growing in popularity among the new generation of retirees coming along in the 21st Century, and I think you will see why.

CHAPTER THIRTEEN

Income Riders on Fixed Index Annuities

"Retirement is like a long vacation in Las Vegas. The goal is to enjoy it the fullest, but not so fully that you run out of money."

~ Jonathan Clements

Anyone seeking a guaranteed income during retirement, one they cannot outlive, should take a look at the newly redesigned annuities the insurance industry offers these days. These revamped vehicles have the attributes of both a savings program and an investment account in that they have the potential to provide market-based returns and offer a guaranteed lifetime income stream with zero risk to your principal — all under the same roof.

Did someone say, "Hold the phone! That sounds too good to be true!"? Well, let's get our magnifying glass and calculator and see how they work.

The product: The product goes by many names — income annuity, hybrid annuity, income growth annuity. You may even hear other names for it, depending on what dialect of financial advisor language you speak. The most popular name for them, however, is *hybrid.* Why hybrid? Because they combine two things: the fixed index annuity (FIA) with a guaranteed lifetime withdrawal benefit (GLWB), which some call an "income rider." We all know what a hybrid automobile is. That's a good way to understand how these hybrid annuities function. The two engines working in sync produces the fuel economy. Likewise, it's the FIA with the GLWB attached that makes this retirement income investment vehicle go.

Another way to think of the hybrid annuity is a motorcycle and a side car. The motorcycle can stand alone, but the sidecar has got to be attached to the bike. You can buy a stand-alone FIA, but you can't buy a rider on its own.

When you mention the word "annuity" to some people, they wrinkle up their nose and want to hurl a brick at you. That's because they haven't kept up with the times. Remember how American-made automobiles used to fall apart? The theme song for Detroit back in the 1950s and 1960s was "Shake, Rattle and Roll." Motor City got the message when American consumers began voting with their pocketbooks. In the 1960s, people started buying Volkswagens, Toyotas and Fiats, and leaving the Fords, Chevys and Chryslers in the showroom. Auto executives started to pay attention to all the complaints about their big and bulky automobiles. They charged their engineers to start designing quality automobiles. Only when American automobile manufacturing plants retooled and began turning out quality cars did the American consumer return to their showrooms.

It was somewhat like that with the insurance industry. In the 1980s, annuities were old-fashioned and were not flying off the shelves. Why? Because they were not very well designed. If you wanted a guaranteed income stream, you had to give the insurance company a lump sum of money and then annuitize the contract. That meant you would receive a payout for a certain number of years, even for the rest of your life if you chose, but you had to completely forfeit control of the money. In other words, if you annuitized your $100,000 traditional fixed annuity, and then died three months later, you got three payments of a few hundred dollars each, and the insurance company kept the rest! Baby boomers just weren't going for that. I don't blame them. I wouldn't recommend one of those to my clients, either.

Then you have *variable* annuities. Stockbrokers sell variable annuities to clients who want to invest in the stock market but wish to have the gains tax-deferred. Variable annuities can lose money, as many who owned them found out in the last stock market crash.

So if someone starts looking around for a blunt instrument like a baseball bat when you mention annuities, it's probably because they, or someone they know, had a bad experience with either variable annuities or old-style annuities. The annuities I am describing here are definitely not those. These were developed in the mid-1990s to address public demand. These new-style hybrid annuities are so made over that they should be given a new name just to stave off confusion. Let's start with why they are called fixed index annuities. We will get to the guaranteed income part later. The term, "fixed index annuity" breaks down this way:

- **FIXED** — Fixed index annuities are the offspring of traditional fixed annuities. They are "fixed" in the sense that the investor's money is safe from market risk. "Fixed" is also the classification by which they are identified by various state departments of insurance, the agencies which regulate such products. With "fixed" annuities, the investor, owner or annuitant in these types of contracts does not actually own any stocks, securities, bonds, mutual funds or any other equity that could potentially go down in value. The investor owns a contract with an insurance company that has certain guarantees. So how, then, does it have market-based returns?

- **INDEX** — Unlike the traditional fixed annuity, which has a declared interest rate adjusted each year, the index annuity's rate of interest is determined by the performance of a stock market index, like the S&P 500, the Nasdaq, the Dow Jones or even a combination of these and other indices, depending on how you set it up. Within the contract there are provisions for tweaking the way interest is credited. Crediting strategy adjustments can be made each year. These vary from company to company. The options are there to accommodate the owner's preference. One year, for example, the owner may feel like the market will perform well and may opt to allow 100 percent of his crediting to track a market index, or perhaps a combination of indices, depending on how the carrier structures the contract. Another year, the owner may opt to be more conservative and split the crediting between the guaranteed fixed interest and a market index. But the basic principle is this: When the index goes up, so does your account value. When the index goes down, your gains are locked in and you do not participate in the downturn. Your account waits for the market to go up and goes up with it. Typically, contract values reset every year. The worst you can do in a declining market is zero growth. Proponents of this strategy, in fact, like to use the expression "**zero is your hero**" in a down market year. Caps are an important element to this method of crediting these accounts. The gains are capped at a level established by the insurance carrier each year. That means, for example, if the S&P 500 index is up 20 percent, your account will grow up to a cap. If the cap is 5 percent, then you will earn 5 percent. If the cap is 10 percent, then you will only get 10 percent. By the same token, if the market nosedives, most contracts offer you a floor. If the floor is 2 percent, then your account will at least come away from that down year with a 2-percent growth. What you have accrued in the account will remain untouched by the falling values of the stock market.

- **ANNUITY** — It is an annuity and meets the standards of an annuity as defined by various state departments of insurance around the country. Returns within the contract are tax-deferred — that is, you don't pay taxes on the gains until you reach in and take the money out in the form of a withdrawal. Like most other annuities, while in deferral, you are typically allowed to withdraw 10 percent from the contract annually without paying surrender penalties. These are sometimes called "free withdrawals" if they are taken while the surrender period (typically 10 years) is still in place. Surrender penalties are like the "penalties for early withdrawals" made famous with bank CDs. Surrender charges vary from company to company. A typical surrender penalty is 12 percent, declining each year of the surrender period until it reaches zero at the end. Surrender periods are typically 10 years, give or take a year or two. Most FIA's are also RMD (Required Minimum Distribution) friendly. Many FIAs allow for larger distributions than 10 percent if the owner is confined to a nursing home or is terminally ill. There is no penalty imposed for any size withdrawal once the contract has passed the surrender period.

The best way to understand the way interest is credited within FIAs is to think of two buckets — a *fixed interest* bucket, like the old-style traditional fixed annuity, and an *index* bucket where the market index determines your gains. You can change the weight of these buckets each year. Each year you can adjust your crediting method. If you put, say, $100,000 into an FIA, you could put half of it in the *fixed* crediting method and the other half in the *index* crediting method, or any combination you felt would work to your advantage.

A further variation on the same theme is the *averaging strategy*. With this strategy, the insurance company would take a snapshot of the market every month for 12 months. At the end of the year they would add it up and divide by 12, which would give you a return based on the *average* of what the market did. Most companies who offer averaging strategies don't have caps, they have spreads. The spread is the percentage the insurance company would take off the top, maybe 5 percent or so. This type of crediting strategy works very well in a choppy market where stock prices fluctuate dramatically and often.

Another variation within the crediting strategies is the *monthly strategy.* This is where the insurance company takes a snapshot of the market each month and gives you a percentage of the growth with each month standing on its own.

It is crucial to understand why these various crediting strategies exist. They are not there just to confuse you. The way to get the most out of one of these financial instruments is to review them with your financial advisor every year and adjust your crediting strategy to fit current market behavior.

I use different strategies to accommodate changes in the market, all within the FIA. One strategy works well when the market is choppy. Another works well when the market is bullish. Another works well when the market is on a downturn. This is a safe way to capitalize on most of the market gains in a bull market and to avoid getting hurt when the bears take over. You get a portion of the market gains but not all of it. The best part is you do not participate in the market losses.

That's basically it for the **fixed index annuity.** Since Americans tend to vote for retirement products with their pocketbooks, as they do with cars, soap or any other product, it is important to note that in 2013, FIA sales were $39.3 billion, an increase of 16 percent over the previous year, according to LIMRA, an insurance research organization. And according to the National Association for Fixed Annuities (NAFA), more than half of all FIAs purchased now include an **income rider,** which makes them *hybrid* annuities, or *income* annuities.

Income Riders

Fixed index annuities can stand alone, of course, and work OK without an income rider, but what a difference it makes when you attach one! The income rider was unveiled by the insurance industry sometime in the mid-2000s as an answer to the annuitizing dilemma. Before the income rider, the only way you could convert your contract to an income stream was to forfeit control of the account balance and settle for a payout, either over a fixed period of time or for life. The only problem with that, of course, was that your heirs got nothing when you died. The income rider fixed all that. Income riders are also called guaranteed lifetime income benefits (GLWBs), guaranteed lifetime income riders (GLIBs) and guaranteed lifetime income riders (GLIRs), but they all serve essentially the same purpose — producing a pension-like income you cannot outlive.

Income riders come with a few moving parts of their own which are separate and distinct from the moving parts of the FIA to which they are attached. Even though their basic function remains the same from carrier to carrier, each company builds its income rider a little differently, it seems. It would be impossible to lay out all the nuances of each here, but consider this a broad-brush explanation. See me personally and I will make sure you know exactly how they function down to the last little detail.

Cost — Income riders aren't free, but they cost very little — usually between 75 basis points (less than 1 percent of the account balance) annually and 1.5 percent of the FIA account balance annually. This cost can be expressed outright or it can sometimes be expressed as returns reduced by that amount. In other words, if the annuity earns 6 percent interest one year and the constant cost of the income rider is 75 bps (basis points), then the net return of the annuity that year would be 5.25 percent.

Guarantee — You may have noticed that acronyms for the income rider all start with the letter "G," and that the "G" stands for "guaranteed." Who guarantees the annuity? The insurance company. Insurance companies have several layers of guarantees:

(a) Reinsurance. Insurance companies actually buy insurance from other insurance companies who specialize in reinsuring insurance contracts.

(b) Legal reserve system. Insurance companies are required to participate in the legal reserve pool of the state in which they do business. That way, if an insurance company fails, other insurance companies buy the failed insurance company's book of business and are bound to carry out the defunct insurance companies promises.

(c) Reserves. This boils down to the claims-paying capability of the insurance company itself, which is why insurance companies have ratings. Unlike banks, insurance companies are required to sequester a certain portion of their assets (set them aside) for payment of claims. These funds are required by law to be in cash or marketable securities and serve to underwrite the company's claims liability. Neither annuities nor income riders are guaranteed by the FDIC.

Long-term care — Some, not all, insurance carriers even provide for the income to increase substantially (double in some cases) if the annuity owner is confined to a nursing home. Some make this coverage more expansive to include other forms of long-term care. Other carriers provide additional riders that can shelter the annuity owner even more from the risks of long-term care expense. The annuity owner typically retains access to the annuity's base account and continues to receive interest credits as the base account grows.

Roll-up rate — When you purchase an income rider, it adds to the contract what is in essence a "ledger" account. This account is sometimes called a "virtual" account, an "income calculation base," a "benefit base" or an "income account." It all serves the same function, however, because it is from this base account (which starts off with the same value as the FIA account balance) that a "roll-up rate" is figured. A roll-up rate is the rate by which this ledger account grows until income is triggered by the annuity owner. The roll-up rate varies from carrier to carrier but common roll-up rates are between 6 and 8 percent. These rates tend to fluctuate with the prevailing interest rate environment, but once they are locked in place, they remain the same until income is triggered or until the end of the roll-up period, which is typically 10 years or more, after which the annuity owner can usually extend the roll-up period again, if desired, at whatever prevailing rate is declared at that time.

Please understand that this ledger account is not the "walk-away" money. The walk-away money, the money you would pocket if you walked away from the contract, is the FIA's actual account value. When tradespeople talk about annuity products, you will sometimes hear expressions such as: "That's a 10-year walk-away annuity." That simply means that after 10 years, there is no surrender charge and you can take your FIA account balance and any earnings that may have accrued during that time and simply walk away. You do not have to annuitize the contract to get your money out of it, in other words, as with certain old-style annuities (probably another reason for the bad rep they sometimes received).

Income — Think of the income stream like a dry riverbed in front of a massive dam. The dam was constructed when you purchased the annuity. The lake behind the dam fills up with interest from the roll-up rate. Naturally, the longer you allow the dam to go untapped, the larger your lake, or your income account, grows.

"But I thought I could never receive that money in a lump sum."

That's right, you can't. But the larger your ledger account becomes, the more income you can draw when you decide to start it. There is a formula for this that varies a bit from carrier to carrier. Typically, if you are between the ages of 60 and 70 years of age, your income will be 5 percent of your "ledger" account per year (paid monthly if you wish). If you start your income between the ages of 70 and 80, you will receive 6 percent of your income base account for life.

With most riders, if the accumulation value (actual account value) is higher than the income account value (calculation base), then you are able to use the higher of the two accounts as a calculation base. Once you trigger the income, that amount is locked in for life. Some companies have optional inflation provisions.

As you can see, income riders have a few moving parts. I can only imagine the discussions that must have taken place in the boardrooms where the details of these products were hammered out. I believe more thought was given to how they work and what they do than to our capacity to understand them, let alone explain them. It reminds me of modern automobiles. They last longer and perform better but gone are the days when you could let just anybody with a rag sticking out of their back pocket work on them. With the exception of changing the oil or replacing windshield wiper blades, I'm taking my car to a manufacturer's certified repair facility.

As detailed as the description offered here is, it is an overview. When someone asks me what time it is, I usually give them the answer in three syllables. They usually don't want to know how a clock works, nor are they expecting me to go into depth about the International Dateline and Greenwich Mean Time. "Three o'clock" will do just fine. When it comes to annuities, however, you need to have a detailed explanation of how they function before you put your money into one. You need to at least know the basic terms in the annuity glossary and have a working knowledge of the annuity's major moving parts and how they affect you. I know I have sometimes irritated some of my clients by explaining more about the decisions they were making than their curiosity demanded, but that is the role of a sensitive and caring financial advisor. You don't really know something, after all, until you can answer the "why and how" questions of a spouse or other close family member.

If you intend to use these financial instruments as part of your retirement income plan, you need to know as much as your curiosity demands. How else will you be able trust them? In all the years I have been helping people make the decisions they are faced with when they see retirement on the horizon, I have never had one come back to me and say, "Sandy, we hate that annuity you recommended." If I think that is a possible eventuality, I find that out way before we cross that river. On the other hand, especially after a big market crash, when some of their friends are crying the blues about their damaged portfolios, I have had plenty of clients come up and offer to give me a hug because they didn't lose any of their life's savings to such a cataclysm as that.

A Case in Point

As a financial counselor, my main job is solving problems. I look into my "toolbox" sometimes to see if I have just the right tool, or financial strategy, to fit the situation. I am neither obligated nor inclined to use one particular insurance company, brokerage firm, concept or combination of strategies over another. In my book, it's a matter of the right tool for the job.

When it comes to these "hybrid" annuities, or "income" annuities, the reason I find myself recommending them more and more in the retirement planning side of my practice is because of what they do. They provide what so many of my clients want and need — guaranteed income for life.

A woman came into my office one morning and was visibly upset. She had just been fired from her job after devoting nearly 30 years to the firm as a loyal employee. She had worked in the accounting department of a large telecom company that had recently fallen on hard times. She was 62 years old. She had planned on retiring when she turned 65, but was now looking for a job and having little success. The woman had been given a small severance package that included a year's salary, but she had to forfeit all claims to a pension that she had been counting on for retirement.

I was seeing little in the way of encouragement until she told me that she had diligently contributed the maximum allowable to her 401(k) for years, and her employer had matched her contributions dollar for dollar. The account was now worth almost $350,000. She did not realize how valuable this would prove to be. We ran the numbers and figured up that if she rolled the 401(k) into an FIA with an income rider, she could retire as planned and never have to work again. The smile that crossed her face was a reminder of why I do what I do.

CHAPTER FOURTEEN

How You Invest in Retirement DOES Make a Difference!

"It's not how much money you make, but how much money you keep, how hard it works for you and how many generations you keep it for."

~ Robert Kiyosaki

The most fascinating thing about butterflies, and what makes them an excellent metaphor for success in life, is they start out as an earthbound worm and end up as a glorious, colorful flying creature that is a marvel to behold.

Earlier in this book, we talked about the changes we go through in our financial lives — the three stages of accumulation, preservation and distribution. Each one of those phases calls for a change in our mindset when it comes to investing.

Just as the caterpillar starts out slow and limited in mobility, we all started out our larval investing stage the same way — with a brokerage house and mutual funds. Before you shake your head no, think about it. If you worked for a company and you participated in a 401(k), you may not have paid much attention, but behind the scenes was a big company like Magellan or Fidelity, who served as a custodian (another word for middleman). This custodian most likely invested your money in mutual funds. These mutual funds had a fund manager who made the trading decisions on a day-by-day basis. There is nothing wrong with that. We had to start somewhere. We had no lump sum of money to invest.

If you were self-employed, you might have used an IRA account. If you are like most folks, you worked through a brokerage house, such as Raymond James, Charles Schwab, Ameriprise, Edward D. Jones... the list goes on. There must be thousands of places that would qualify as brokerage houses where they sell stocks, bonds, mutual funds and variable annuities. You put your money with the broker and you saved and invested as the years went by.

Over the years, the market went up and down, but overall there was growth. The exception to that is what market watchers call the "lost decade," which began in 2000. The market had plenty of ups and downs, but if you flattened them all out, you were, roughly speaking, back where you started. To a young investor with time on his or her side, this may not be a big deal. But if you are in your 50s and 60s, it's a big deal. The closer you are to retirement, you need to capture as much of the market gains as possible and avoid the losses, or if you do lose some of it, you want to keep those losses small.

When these brokers put you in mutual funds, it seemed like a good idea at the time. It was a way to spread out your investments, help you diversify. If you were like most young investors, it was a little like ordering a meal in a restaurant. You placed your order for the mutual fund with your broker and didn't ask questions about the ingredients or how the entrée was prepared. Here's an example of the ingredients of a mutual fund:

A mutual fund has a ratio of equities (stocks) to bonds. Let's say you have a mutual fund with ratio of 70 percent stocks and 30 percent bonds. As the market goes up you are happy. When the market goes down, you are not so happy. When that happens, the bonds will stabilize, and the stocks will lose value. When you were younger, you had time to ride the market up and down. But if you are in your 50s and 60s, time is condensed.

Don't get me wrong... mutual funds are great for what they do. They got you to where you are right now, and they may continue to play a part in your overall investment portfolio. But if you are at that wonderful age where you start getting subscription notices for AARP and McDonald's offers you senior coffee, then there are some tweaks that you must make in your investing — simply because of where you are in the stream of time. That is unless, of course, you don't want to become a butterfly and would prefer to remain a caterpillar, in which case you may just skip the rest of the chapter.

If you remain in this larval stage of investing, you are saddled by the unwieldy nature of mutual funds. You can't move in and out of them like you can individual stocks. To sell out of them, you must wait until the end of the business day and you would have to sell your shares in that mutual fund at whatever they are worth at that day's closing bell. It is virtually impossible for you to react quickly enough in a volatile market. By the time you have locked in your trade, the market will have changed. Then there are the fees associated with mutual funds. The prospectus discloses some of the fees but not all of them, and these hidden costs can eat up your gains. The bottom line is simply this: brokers and brokerage houses do not allow you to minimize losses and maximize gains as you need to do when you are approaching retirement.

Institutional vs. Individual Investing

What is institutional investing versus individual investing? It boils down to bypassing the entire process of using brokerage houses and broker-dealers and plugging in directly to the fund manager. Gone are the delays and the fees, charges and costs (hidden and otherwise) that come right off the top of your returns. Some people refer to it as "wholesale" versus "retail" investing.

To use our firm, Sandy Morris Financial Services, as an example, the team that I use manages a portfolio worth more than $1.7 billion. Our team consists of 10 individual skilled money managers who spend their entire day watching what I call "Bloomberg monitors" that tell them the second-by-second movements of the stock market. These teams manage money for banks, investment companies, insurance companies and large corporations. There was a time when these institutional-level money managers did not allow the private sector to drink from their well and Investment Advisor Representatives like me could not offer institutional investing to their clients. A team does the buying and trading under the direction of a chief financial officer.

These money managers use several investing models, and this is the key ingredient that makes this a superior system for retired or retiring investors. Each model is used for various investing goals. These investment models range from conservative to more growth-oriented. They can even design one specifically for the individual client, if necessary. Let's say that the conservative model contains 20–30 percent bonds and 50–60 percent stocks and the rest is in emerging markets and alternative investments. When the investment team senses that the market is advancing, they don't have to wait until the close of business to make a move. They instantly shift the emphasis of that model to add more weight to the equities to take advantage of the market surge. By the same token, if the market reverses, they go the opposite direction. Institutional investors have much more flexibility than do individual investors. While you are out golfing, playing with the grandchildren or just relaxing on the beach, these professionals are watching the market in real time and are taking a proactive versus a reactive position when it comes to investing your money.

Finding the Sweet Spot

In golf, the club head has a quarter-sized sweet spot. The perfect golf swing connects the sweet spot of the club head with the ball dead center, giving the golf ball a long, true shot down the fairway. When you were a young investor and time was on your side, projections were acceptable in the planning process. As you advance toward retirement, however, you are more interested in the word *"guarantee."* As good as institutional investing is, you can't put the word "guarantee" with it. The stock market, no matter how you shake it, comes with a degree of risk that can be controlled but not completely mitigated.

Since most of my clients are approaching retirement or are already retired, I interview them carefully to see where and in what combination it is best to place their assets between market-based institutional investments and guaranteed investments, such as the hybrid annuities mentioned in the previous chapter. Which direction the plan takes is entirely up to the client. While most people who are on the threshold of retirement want guaranteed incomes and guaranteed principle, they also want the most growth possible as well. There is truly no one-size-fits-all for this. In the 12 years I have been helping clients devise retirement income plans, I cannot think of one plan that was exactly like another. Each one is as unique as the thumbprint of the person owning it.

ABOUT THE AUTHOR

Sandy Morris lives and works in Tampa, Florida, an area she has called home for 21 years and that some people call the "left coast" of the Sunshine State. If you detect a touch of honeysuckle and down-home sunshine in her accent, it's because she grew up in the small town of Wickliffe, Kentucky, located in the western tip of the state where the Ohio and Mississippi rivers meet.

In 2002, Sandy founded Sandy Morris Financial & Estate Planning Services, a full-service financial advisory firm of which she is president and chief operating officer. The firm started out with just her and now has a large staff and several thousand clients in the bustling Tampa Bay and Sarasota area. SMF&EPS specializes in tax efficient investment, income and estate planning. Sandy is an investment advisor and a Certified Estate Planner, planning tax efficient income, tax saving planning and estate planning. She has been featured in Forbes magazine and has been interviewed by several radio and television stations, including CBS television and WFLA News Radio 970.

Personal Journey

By her account of things, Sandy's early life was not one of privilege and ease. As a young girl she worked on a farm. The life lessons she learned growing up helped shape the self-reliant yet caring character that she would later exhibit in her professional life.

Openness defines Sandy's personality. She is candid when talking about her family, which she says had a significant influence on her life. She says she had a healthy fear of her father, who was a strict disciplinarian, but the experience taught her how important it is to be resourceful and that all excuses are equal.

"He enforced a zero-tolerance policy for excuses at our house," Sandy says. "I remember as a little girl helping him work on machinery. If he asked me to go get a screwdriver, I knew better than to ask whether he wanted a flat-head or a Phillips. I got both, and every size of each, and ran when I brought them to him. He was a John Wayne kind of man — tall and authoritative. He used to say, 'Use your head for something other than a place to hang a hat.'" Her father, Billy Patterson, died at the age of 80.

Her mother, Sherry Hawf, was a teenager when she gave birth to Sandy. "We were more like sisters than mother and daughter," Sandy says, adding that while her father hardened her to the realities of life and made her tough, it was her mother, her grandmother and her stepsisters who engendered the softer side in her as she matured.

Sandy cherishes her relationship with her adult son, her daughter-in-law and her two grandchildren, Hunter and Bristol.

Sandy recounts how blessed she was to have many mentors in her journey to success.

"Jim Rhome provided me with my first exposure to personal development," says Sandy. "He taught me about the seasons in each area of life and how to recognize them and plan accordingly."

Others who contributed to her development as a professional include Zig Ziglar, Bryan Tracy, Dr. Joe Vitale, and Mark Victor Hansen.

"I was like a sponge around them," says Sandy. "I soaked up all I could. I adopted their philosophy of success — 'Help enough people get what they want in life and what you want in life will come to you.'"

Sandy also adds Larry Thompson, one of the founders of Herbalife, to her list of mentors. It was Larry who taught her how to implement a daily method of operation and utilize the concept of time management.

Sandy found herself arriving at financial success in her early 40s but felt something was missing.

"I wondered what all the 'hoopla' was about," she recalls. "Having houses, cars, boats, jewelry and worldly possessions most people only dream of just left me wondering what was my purpose. What's next? I'm in my 40s — is this all there is?"

Sandy found that she didn't have the energy or time to even take care of all the things she had acquired. Instead of running her life, she felt as if life was running her. She first met Tony Robbins, a motivational speaker, self-help author and life coach, when she was 24. At the time, she had no money and had sold some personal items to come up with the money to pay for one of his workshops.

"His workshops changed my life," Sandy says, adding that from time to time she referred back to them for direction as she continued her journey of success.

From Low Point to High Point

One Sunday morning Sandy found herself barely having the energy to get out of bed. She had become completely exhausted both physically and emotionally. She was so bone weary that she wondered if she had some dreadful sickness. She found out later that it was adrenal fatigue, brought on by prolonged stress. It was during that low point in her life that she said aloud, "God, I need divine intervention." She remembered the spiritually uplifting quality of Tony Robbins' words and began wondering where he was these days.

"Sometimes when you ask for something at your lowest ebb, the answer comes quickly," says Sandy, adding that she has learned to listen for what she calls "that whisper" that follows a request for divine guidance. She typed in the words Tony Robbins in the Google search bar and learned that the dynamic speaker was to appear the next weekend in nearby Fort Lauderdale, Florida.

She collected her mother and the two of them got the closest seat to the front of the stage so they wouldn't miss a word. Sandy became what is known as a "platinum partner" of Robbins' organization and traveled throughout the world to his rallies and speaking events that next year, "soaking up all I could."

"The biggest questions of my life were answered," Sandy recalls. "Why am I here? What is my purpose?"

Sandy says the answer lay in service to others.

"Like many who achieve financial success but find themselves empty with nothing to look forward to, I had learned to value what those around me valued," says Sandy. Her focus had become acquiring the trappings of power and success.

At one particular Tony Robbins workshop in Australia, Sandy says that saw that her highest value is LOVE.

"I realized that I was really good at one thing — making others feel safe and giving them certainty in life," says Sandy. "It became my purpose in life for the first time. Instead of working for a living, I get up every day to serve — help as many others people as possible find certainty in their lives.

Sandy has continued to be a proponent of reading good books. "I don't know where I would be without books," she says. "Books helped me any time I faced a challenge or needed to understand the details of some new undertaking."

Professional Mission

Sandy is driven by a strong desire to help others and places a strong emphasis on providing financial education to seniors, thereby giving them the tools they need to make good decisions.

"This is the juice that keeps me going," she says.

Sandy hosts a radio talk show and is often called upon to speak on the subject of retirement planning at public events. She says with a laugh that she sometimes wonders what that shy, freckle-faced schoolgirl with braces is doing behind the microphone or in front of an audience of such magnitude. She acknowledges that her life — while it has not been easy — continues to be a grand *adventure!*

ACKNOWLEDGEMENTS

I would like to thank the founders of Advisors Excel for providing me the platform from which I was able to write this book, and their creative team members, who are all top-notch professionals. Thanks also to all of my industry associates for writing their books. They inspired and motivated me to finish my mine.

I am grateful to my immediate family for all of their love, admiration, support and continued encouragement. It's amazing what we will do to keep from disappointing our family.

I would be remiss if I did not acknowledge the love of my life, my husband, Joe, for the phrase he spoke to me many years ago: "I've never known anyone who has become as successful as you without a college education." He has no idea how much that inspired me.

Lastly, and most importantly, my only child, Clinton. What can I say? I'm a blessed mother, to be given a son like him. He keeps me grounded and constantly reminds me of what's most important in life — LOVE — which is his greatest value. It took me almost 50 years to figure that one out! Thank you, son.